Exam Success

2357 NVQ Diploma in Electrotechnical Technology

First published 2011

© 2011 The City and Guilds of London Institute

City & Guilds is a trademark of the City and Guilds of London Institute

ISBN: 978-0-85193-197-5

Cover and book design by CDT Design Ltd
Typeset by Select Typesetters Ltd
Edited by Mary Groom
Printed in the UK by Nuffield Press

With thanks to Peter Tanner

Exam Success
2357 NVQ Diploma in Electrotechnical Technology

City & Guilds Level 3 NVQ Diploma in Electrotechnical Technology (2357)

City & Guilds is the UK's leading provider of
vocational qualifications, offering over 500
awards across a wide range of industries, and
progressing from entry level to the highest
levels of professional achievement. With over
8500 centres in 100 countries, City & Guilds
is recognised by employers worldwide for
providing qualifications that offer proof of
the skills they need to get the job done.

For publication enquiries:
City & Guilds
1 Giltspur Street
London EC1A 9DD
T +44 (0)844 543 0000
Email centresupport@cityandguilds.com
www.cityandguilds.com/publications

Queries or feedback on any of our
publications should be sent to
publishingfeedback@cityandguilds.com.

Contents

Introduction

How to use this book

This book has been written as an exam practice aid for some of the exams you will need to take to complete the City & Guilds Level 3 NVQ Diploma in Electrotechnical Technology (2357). It sets out methods of studying, offers advice on exam preparation and provides details of the scope and structure of the examinations, alongside sample questions with fully worked-through answers. Used as a study guide for exam preparation and practice, it will help you to reinforce and test your existing knowledge, and will give you guidelines and advice about sitting the exam. You should try to answer the sample test questions under exam conditions (or as close as you can get) and then review all of your answers. This will help you to become familiar with the types of question that might be asked in the exam and will also give you an idea of how to pace yourself in order to complete all questions comfortably within the time limit. This book cannot guarantee a positive exam result, but it can play an important role in your overall revision programme, enabling you to focus your preparation and approach the exam with confidence.

City & Guilds Level 3 NVQ Diploma in Electrotechnical Technology (2357)

The qualification you are taking is for learners in England, Wales and Northern Ireland who want to work as an electrician, installing systems and equipment in buildings, structures and the environment within the electrotechnical industry. It allows you to learn, develop and practise the skills required for employment and/or career progression in the electrotechnical sector. It contributes knowledge, understanding, and practical skills regarding installing electrotechnical systems and equipment. Once you have learnt the required skills and knowledge you will demonstrate your occupational competence in the workplace within this qualification. The 2357 qualification is part of the SummitSkills Electrotechnical Apprenticeship framework and provides a nationally recognised QCF qualification for the electrotechnical industry.

This qualification is divided into two routes:
– City & Guilds Level 3 NVQ Diploma in Installing Electrotechnical Systems and Equipment (Buildings, Structures and the Environment) (2357-13/91)
– City & Guilds Level 3 NVQ Diploma in Electrotechnical Services (Electrical Maintenance) (2357-23/92)

Notes

Throughout the qualification you will be assessed by various different methods, including observation of practical tasks, assignments and online and short answer tests.

This book contains one practice exam for each of the following four assessments:
– Unit 301 GOLA online multiple choice test
– Unit 305 GOLA online multiple choice test
– Unit 309 GOLA online multiple choice test
– Unit 309 Short answer paper

Finding a centre
In order to take the exams, you must be registered at an approved City & Guilds centre for the 2357 qualification. You can find your nearest centre by looking up the qualification number 2357 on www.cityandguilds.com.

Awarding and reporting
When you complete the City & Guilds 2357 NVQ Diploma online examinations, you will be given your provisional results, as well as a breakdown of your performance in the various areas of the examination. This is a useful diagnostic tool if you fail the exam, as it enables you to identify your individual strengths and weaknesses across the different topics.

A certificate is issued automatically when you have been successful in the assessment, but it will not indicate a grade or percentage pass. Your centre will receive your Notification of Candidate's Results and Certificate. Any correspondence is conducted through the centre. The centre will also receive consolidated results lists detailing the performance of all candidates entered.

If you have particular requirements that will affect your ability to attend and take the examination, then your centre should refer to the City & Guilds policy document 'Access to Assessment: Candidates with Particlar Requirements'.

The exams

The exams

Notes

The exams

This book covers three multiple choice exams and one short answer paper that you will need to sit as part of your assessment for the 2357 NVQ Diploma.

There are three online multiple choice exams, with each examination containing a different number of questions based on the topic area of the unit. The exams are therefore of varying duration (details are shown below). The tests are offered on GOLA, a simple online service that does not require strong IT skills. GOLA uses a bank of questions set and approved by City & Guilds. Each candidate receives randomised questions, so no two candidates will sit exactly the same test.

There is also a short answer paper for Unit 309. This will be sat under exam conditions as a written paper.

City & Guilds number	Unit title	No. of questions	Duration (mins.)	Type of exam
301	Understanding health and safety legislation, practices and procedures (Installing and maintaining electrotechnical systems and equipment)	15	30	Online GOLA
305	Understanding the practices and procedures for the preparation and installation of wiring systems and electrotechnical equipment in buildings, structures and the environment	15	30	Online GOLA
309	Understanding the electrical principles associated with the design, building, installation and maintenance of electrical equipment and systems	30	60	Online GOLA
309	Understanding the electrical principles associated with the design, building, installation and maintenance of electrical equipment and systems	30	120	Short answer paper

The exams for Units 301 and 309 are operated as closed-book examinations, which means you cannot take any reference materials into the exam with you. For the exam for Unit 305, you are allowed to take a clean copy of BS 7671 (IEE Wiring Regulations) into the exam with you. For the two exams for Unit 309, you are allowed to use a calculator.

Sitting a City & Guilds online examination

The test will be taken under usual exam conditions. You will not be able to refer to any materials or publications, other than BS 7671 (IEE Wiring Regulations) for Unit 305. If you leave the exam room unaccompanied before the end of the test period, you may not be allowed to come back into the exam.

When you take a City & Guilds test online, you can go through a tutorial to familiarise yourself with the online procedures. When you are logged on to take the exam, the first screen will give you the chance to go into a tutorial. The tutorial shows how the exam will be presented and how to get help, how to move between different screens, and how to mark questions that you want to return to later.

Please work through the tutorial before you start your examination.

This will show you how to answer questions and use the menu options to help you complete the examination.

Please note that examination conditions now apply.

The time allowed for the tutorial is 10 minutes.

Click on Continue to start the tutorial or Skip to go straight to the examination.

Skip	Continue

Notes

The sample questions in the tutorial are unrelated to the exam you are taking. The tutorial will take 10 minutes, and is not included in the test time. The test will only start once you have completed or skipped the tutorial. A screen will appear that gives the exam information (the time, number of questions and name of the exam).

Examination: 2382-10 Requirements for Electrical Installations

Number of questions: 60

Time allowed: 120 minutes

Note: Examination conditions now apply.

The next screen that will appear is the Help screen, which will give you instructions on how to navigate through this examination. Please click OK to view the Help screen.

The time allowed for the examination will start after you have left the Help screen.

A warning message will appear 5 minutes before the end of the examination.

OK

After clicking 'OK', the Help screen will appear. Clicking the 'Help' button on the tool bar at any time during the exam will recall this screen.

Help Screen

Select your answers from the options displayed. Your answer is stored when you move to another question.

 indicates a selected option. To clear your selection, click the selected option again or select a different option.

Use your mouse to select the command buttons at the top of the screen. Active buttons are bright. If a command button is dim, it is unavailable.

Clicking this...	Does this...	Clicking this...	Does this...
 Time	The time remaining is shown in the bottom right-hand corner. Clicking on the icon displays or hides the time.	 **Previous**	Moves you back to the previous question.
 Help	The Help facility is available throughout the examination.	 **Next**	Moves you forward to the next question.
 Review	Displays a window that enables you to review questions already viewed, indicating those answered and marked. To review all items, ensure the 'view marked questions only' checkbox is unchecked. Double-click on the question number to go to the question you want to review.	 **Exhibit**	Displays a window containing additional information needed to answer the question. Close the 'Exhibit' to return to the question.
 Mark	Flags the current question for review. The button appears light if the question is marked. The question can then be reviewed later by selecting it from the review window.	 **Quit**	Exits the examination.

[OK]

After clicking 'OK' while in the Help screen, the exam timer will start and you will see the first question. The question number is always shown in the lower left-hand corner of the screen. If you answer a question but wish to return to it later, then you can click the 'Flag' button. When you get to the end of the test, you can choose to review these flagged questions.

Notes

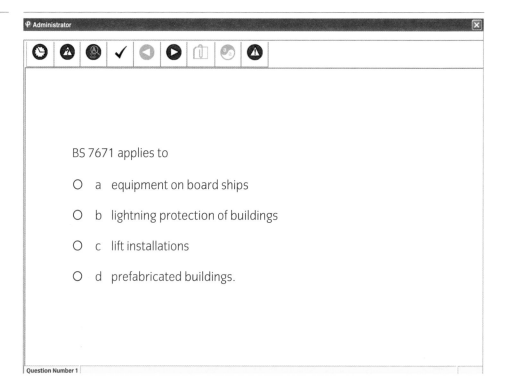

If you select 'Quit' on the tool bar at any point, you will be given the choice of ending the test. **If you select 'Yes', you will not be able to go back to your test.**

If you click 'Time' on the tool bar at any point, the time that you have left will appear in the bottom right-hand corner. When the exam timer counts down to five minutes remaining, a warning will flash on to the screen.

Some of the questions in the test may be accompanied by pictures. The question will tell you whether you will need to click on the 'Exhibit' button to view an image.

When you reach the final question and click 'Next', you will reach a screen that allows you to 'Review your answers' or 'Continue' to end the test. You can review all of your answers or only the ones you have flagged. To review all your answers, make sure that the 'view marked questions only' checkbox is unchecked (click to uncheck). After you have completed your review, you can click 'Continue' to end the test.

Notes

You have answered   30   questions out of a total of   30

To check your answers and return to the examination, click on the Review button. If your time has expired, you cannot return to the examination.

If you wish to submit your answers and end the examination, please click the Continue button.

Clicking Continue will end the examination.

Review | Continue

Once you choose to end the exam by clicking 'Continue', the 'Test completed' screen will appear. Click on 'OK' to end the exam.

Notes

At the end of the exam, you will be given an 'Examination Score Report'. This gives a provisional grade (pass or fail) and breakdown of score by section. This shows your performance in a bar chart and in percentage terms, which allows you to assess your own strengths and weaknesses. If you did not pass, it gives valuable feedback on which areas of the course you should revise before re-sitting the exam.

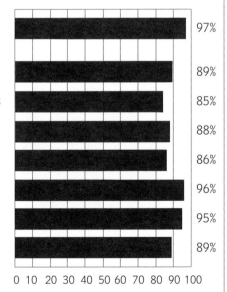

Examination Score Report

Candidate: John Smith

Enrolment No: nav0001

Centre: City & Guilds UK Test Centre 1

Centre No: wow483

Examination: 2382-10 Requirements for Electrical Installations

Provisional grade: Pass

Breakdown of score by section

Section	Score
01 Scope, object and fundamental principles	97%
02 Definitions	89%
03 Assessment of general characteristics	85%
04 Protection for safety	88%
05 Selection and erection of equipment	86%
06 Inspection and testing	96%
07 Special installations or locations	95%
08 Use of appendices	89%

0 10 20 30 40 50 60 70 80 90 100

This chart provides feedback to show candidate performance for each section of the test.
It should be used along with the Test Specification, which can be found in the Scheme Handbook.

Frequently asked questions

When can I sit the papers?
You can sit the exams at any time, as there are no set exam dates. You may need to check with your centre when it is able to hold exam sessions.

Can I use any reference books in the test?
The exams for Units 301 and 309 are operated as closed-book examinations, which means you cannot take any reference materials into the exam with you. For the exam for Unit 305, you are allowed to take a clean copy of BS 7671 (IEE Wiring Regulations) into the exam with you.

Do I have a time limit for taking the test?
Yes, each exam is of a varying duration.

Do I need to be good at IT to do the test online?
No, the system is really easy to use, and you can practise before doing the test.

What happens if the computer crashes in the middle of my online test?
This is unlikely, because of the way the system has been designed. If there is some kind of power or system failure, then your answers will be saved and you can continue on another machine if necessary.

Can people hack into the system and cheat?
There are lots of levels of security built into the system to ensure its safety. Also, each person gets a different set of questions, which makes it very difficult to cheat.

Can I change my answer in the online test?
Yes, you can change your answers quickly, easily and clearly at any time in the test up to the point where you end the exam. With any answers you feel less confident about, you can click the 'Flag' button, which means you can review these questions before you end the test.

How do I know how long I've got left to complete the online test?
You can check the time remaining at any point during the exam by clicking on the 'Time' icon in the tool bar. The time remaining will come up on the bottom right corner of the screen.

Is there only one correct answer (A, B, C or D) to multiple-choice questions?
Yes.

Notes

What happens if I don't answer all of the questions in the online test?

You should attempt to answer all of the questions. If you find a question difficult, mark it using the 'Flag' button and return to it later.

What grades of pass are there?

For all the exams, you can only achieve either a pass or a fail.

When can I resit the test if I fail?

You can resit the exam at any time, and as soon as you and your tutor decide it is right for you, subject to the availability of the online examination or your centre being able to schedule the written test.

Exam content

To help you to fully understand the exam content and what you will be tested on, this section details the learning outcomes that will be assessed for each exam.

Unit 301

Understanding health and safety legislation, practices and procedures (Installing and maintaining electrotechnical systems and equipment)

Duration
30 mins

Type of exam
Online GOLA exam

The areas covered in this exam are:

Syllabus ref	Assessment criteria The learner can...	No. of questions
01.01	specify their own roles and responsibilities and those of others with regard to current relevant legislation	1
01.02	specify particular health and safety risks which may be present and the requirements of current health and safety legislation for the range of electrotechnical work operations	1
02.01	state the procedures that should be followed in the case of accidents which involve injury, including requirements for the treatment of electric shock/electrical burns	1
02.03	state the limitations of their responsibilities in terms of health and safety in the workplace	1
02.04	state the actions to be taken in situations which exceed their level of responsibility for health and safety in the workplace	1
02.05	state the procedures that should be followed in accordance with the relevant health and safety regulations for reporting health, safety and/or welfare issues in the workplace	1
02.06	specify appropriate responsible persons to whom health and safety and welfare related matters should be reported	1
03.03	describe the procedures that should be taken to remove or minimize risks before deciding PPE is needed	1
03.04	state the purpose of PPE	1
03.06	state the first aid facilities that must be available in the work area in accordance with health and safety regulations	1

Notes

03.08	describe safe working practices and procedures	1
04.01	identify warning signs for the seven main groups of hazardous substance	1
04.02	define what is meant by the term hazard in relation to health and safety legislation in the workplace	1
04.07	explain situations where asbestos may be encountered	1
04.08	specify the procedures for dealing with the suspected presence of asbestos in the workplace	1
Total		**15**

Unit 305

Understanding the practices and procedures for the preparation and installation of wiring systems and electrotechnical equipment in buildings, structures and the environment

Duration
30 mins

Type of exam
Online GOLA exam

The areas covered in this exam are:

Syllabus ref	Assessment criteria The learner can...	No. of questions
07.01	specify the main requirements of the following topics in accordance with the current version of the IEE Wiring Regulations and describe how they impact upon the installation of wiring systems, associated equipment and enclosures:	
07.01.a	Protection against electric shock	3
07.01.b	Protection against fire, flammable situations and explosive atmospheres	2
07.01.c	Selection and erection of equipment and segregation	4
07.01.d	Isolation and switching	2
07.01.e	Special locations	4
Total		**15**

Unit 309
Understanding the electrical principles associated with the design, building, installation and maintenance of electrical equipment and systems

Duration
60 mins/1 hour

Type of exam
Online GOLA exam

The areas covered in this exam are:

Syllabus ref	Assessment criteria The learner can...	No. of questions
01.01	identify and apply appropriate mathematical principles which are relevant to electrotechnical work tasks	2
02.01	identify and use internationally recognised (SI) units of measurement for general variables	2
02.02	identify and determine values of basic SI units which apply specifically to electrical variables	2
02.03	identify appropriate electrical instruments for the measurement and calculation of different electrical values	2
03.01	specify what is meant by mass and weight	1
03.02	explain the principles of basic mechanics as they apply to levers, gears and pulleys	2
03.03	describe the main principles of the following and their inter-relationships: • force • work • energy (kinetic and potential) • power • efficiency	2
03.04	calculate values of electrical energy, power and efficiency	2
04.01	describe the basic principles of electron theory	1
04.02	identify and differentiate between materials which are good conductors and insulators	2
04.03	state the types and properties of different electrical cables	1

04.04	describe what is meant by resistance and resistivity in relation to electrical circuits	2
04.05	explain the relationship between current, voltage and resistance in parallel and series d.c. circuits	1
04.06	calculate the values of current, voltage and resistance in parallel and series d.c. circuits	4
04.07	calculate values of power in parallel and series d.c. circuits	2
04.08	state what is meant by the term voltage drop in relation to electrical circuits	1
04.09	describe the chemical and thermal effects of electrical currents	1
Total		**30**

Notes

Unit 309

Understanding the electrical principles associated with the design, building, installation and maintenance of electrical equipment and systems

Duration

120 mins/2 hours

Type of exam

Short answer paper

The areas covered in this exam are:

Syllabus ref	Assessment criteria The learner can...	No. of questions
05.01	describe the magnetic effects of electrical currents in terms of: • production of a magnetic field • force on a current-carrying conductor in a magnetic field • electromagnetism • electromotive force	1
05.02	describe the basic principles of generating an a.c. supply in terms of: • a single-loop generator • sine-wave • frequency • e.m.f • magnetic flux	1
05.03	explain how the following characteristics of a sine-wave effect the values of a.c. voltage and current: • Root Mean Square (RMS) values • average value	1
06.01	describe how electricity is generated and transmitted for domestic and industrial/commercial consumption	1
06.02	specify the features and characteristics of a generation and transmission system including: • power stations – fossil fuel; hydro; oil; nuclear • super-grid and standard grid system • tranformers • transmission voltages • sub-stations • above and below ground distribution	1
06.03	explain how electricity is generated from other sources	1

06.04	describe the main characteristics of: • single phase electrical supplies • three phase electrical supplies • three phase and neutral supplies • earth-fault loop path • star and delta connections	1
06.05	describe the operating principles, applications and limitations of transformers	1
06.06	state the different types of transformer that are used in electrical supply and distribution networks	1
06.07	determine by calculation and measurement: • primary and secondary voltages • primary and secondary current • kVA rating of a transformer	1
07.01	explain the relationship between resistance, inductance, capacitance and impedance	1
07.02	calculate unknown values of resistance, inductance, inductive reactance, capacitance, capacitive reactance and impedance	1
07.03	explain the relationship between kW, kVAr, kVA and power factor	1
07.04	calculate power factor	1
07.05	explain what is meant by: • power factor correction • load balancing (neutral current)	1
07.06	specify methods of power factor correction	1
07.07	determine the neutral current in a three-phase and neutral supply	1
07.08	calculate values of voltage and current in star and delta connected systems	1
08.01	state the basic types, applications and describe the operating principles of d.c. machines: • series • shunt • compound	1
08.02	describe the operating principles of: • single phase a.c. motors (capacitor start, induction start, universal) • three phase a.c. motors (squirrel cage; wound-rotor) • inverter motor/variable frequency drive • synchronous motors	1

Notes

08.03	state the basic types, applications and limitations of: • single phase a.c. motors (capacitor start, induction start, universal) • three phase a.c. motors (squirrel cage; wound-rotor) • inverter motor/variable frequency drive • synchronous motors	1
08.04	describe the operating principles, limitations and applications of motor control, including: • direct-on-line • star-delta • rotor-resistance • soft-start • variable frequency	1

09.01	specify the main types and operating principles of the following electrical components:
	• contactors
	• relays
	• solenoids
	• over-current protection devices
	  – fuses (HRC, cartridge and re-wireable)
	  – circuit-breakers
	• RCDs
	• RCBOs
		1

09.02	describe how the following components are applied in electrical systems/equipment and state their limitations:
	• contactors
	• relays
	• solenoids
	• over-current protection devices
	  – fuses (HRC, cartridge and re-wireable)
	  – circuit-breakers
	• RCDs
	• RCBOs
		1

10.01	explain the basic principles of illumination and state the applications of: • inverse square law • cosine law • Lumen method	1
10.02	explain the operating principles, types , limitations and applications of luminaires	1
11.01	explain the basic principles of electrical space heating and electrical water heating	1
11.02	explain the operating principles, types , limitations and applications of electrical space and water heating appliances and components	1

12.01	describe the function and application of electronic components that are used in electrotechnical systems	1
12.02	state the basic operating principles and applications of electronic components	1
Total		**30**

Notes

Notes

Tips from the examiner

The following tips are intended to aid confident test performance. Some are more general and would apply to most exams. Others are more specific.

✔ If you rarely use a computer, try to get some practice beforehand. You need to be able to use a mouse to move a cursor arrow around a computer screen, as you will use the cursor to click on the correct answer in the online exam.

✔ Make the most of the learning that you will complete before taking the exams. Try to attend all sessions and be prepared to devote time outside the class to revise for your exams.

✔ On the day of the exam, allow plenty of time for travel to the centre and arrive at the place of the exam at least ten minutes before it's due to start so that you have time to relax and get into the right frame of mind.

✔ Listen carefully to the instructions given by the invigilator.

✔ Read the question and every option carefully before making your selection or starting to write.

✔ Do not rush – there should be plenty of time to answer all the questions.

✔ Attempt to answer all the questions. If a question is not answered, it is marked as wrong. Making an educated guess improves your chances of choosing the correct answer. Remember, if you don't select or write an answer, you will definitely get no marks for that question.

✔ Don't worry about answering the questions in the order in which they appear in the online exam. Choose the 'Flag' option on the tool bar to annotate the questions you want to come back to. If you spend too much time on questions early on, you may not have time to answer the later questions, even though you know the answers.

✔ It is not recommended that you memorise any of the material presented here in the hope it will come up in the exam. The exam questions featured in this book will help you to gauge the kinds of questions that might be asked. It is highly unlikely you will be asked any identical questions in the exam, but you may see variations on certain themes.

Exam practice 1

Exam practice 1

Sample test: Unit 301

The sample test below has 15 questions, the same number as the online exam, and its structure follows that of the online exam. The test appears first without answers, so you can use it as a mock exam. It is then repeated with worked-through answers and comments. Finally, there is an answer key for easy reference.

Answer the questions by filling in the circle next to your chosen option.

1 The Electricity at Work Regulations is a

- a   statutory document which relates to employees only
- b   non-statutory document which relates to employers only
- c   statutory document which relates to employers and employees
- d   non-statutory document relating to employers and employees.

2 To minimise the risk when others are working at height in the same location, the most appropriate item of PPE to be worn would be

- a   a high-visibility jacket
- b   ear defenders
- c   a hard hat
- d   gloves.

3 All accidents at work which involve hospitalisation for more than three days must be reported as part of

- a   RODER
- b   RIDDOR
- c   RIDER
- d   RUDDER.

4 If a trainee electrician, while working on a construction site, notices a live conductor which is exposed to touch, the trainee should

- a   tape it up
- b   report it to a supervisor immediately
- c   short out the ends causing the fuse to blow
- d   write a report on the incident and post it to the office.

5 When a hazard is identified in the workplace, an employee <u>must</u>

- ○ a report the hazard at the next safety briefing
- ○ b mention it if an accident occurs
- ○ c report it immediately to a supervisor
- ○ d write it down and post a report to the office.

6 The <u>main</u> purpose for having a visitors' book in a workplace is to

- ○ a provide data to the police on people's movements
- ○ b account for all persons in the event of an emergency
- ○ c keep records in case items are stolen
- ○ d restrict access to people who have not got hard hats.

7 If an electrician discovers an item of PPE is faulty, the item should be returned, for replacement, to the

- ○ a electrician's employer
- ○ b Health and Safety Executive
- ○ c union representative
- ○ d customer or one of their representatives.

8 PPE should be selected for a particular task

- ○ a as a substitution for minimising any risks
- ○ b following actions to reduce the risks
- ○ c because reducing the risks would be too expensive
- ○ d as a quick means to avoid reducing the risks.

9 The <u>main</u> purpose of visors on hard hats, used when drilling, is to

- ○ a provide magnified vision
- ○ b provide noise protection
- ○ c protect the eyes from debris
- ○ d protect eyes from solar radiation.

10 When passing metal conduit to a colleague who is working on a tower scaffold, correct PPE <u>must</u> include

- ○ a gloves, boots and a hard hat
- ○ b gloves, boots and a face mask
- ○ c boots, face mask and a hard hat
- ○ d face mask, hard hat and gloves.

11 Access by medical crews is an important consideration when selecting the location of a

○ a   fire alarm indicator panel
○ b   car park
○ c   store room
○ d   first aid treatment room.

12 Which one of the following arrangements would comply with current safety guidelines when using a ladder as a means of access to the flat roof on a building?

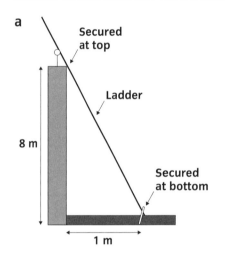

a

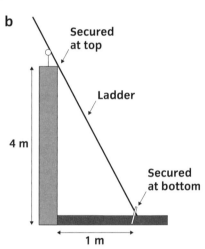

b

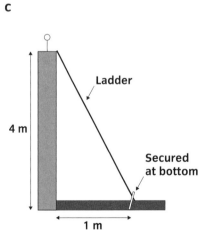

c

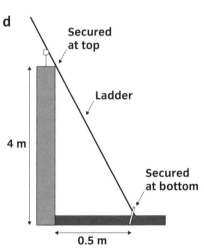

d

○ a
○ b
○ c
○ d

13 The warning sign shown below indicates a danger of

- ○ a   cable fires
- ○ b   oxidising chemicals
- ○ c   tunnel fires
- ○ d   exploding chemicals.

14 Which one of the following is the <u>most</u> likely hazard when drilling 8 mm holes in a plastered wall, 1200 mm above the floor in a domestic dwelling?

- ○ a   Drilling into buried cables.
- ○ b   Falling from a height.
- ○ c   Debris falling from above.
- ○ d   Handling chemicals.

15 Which one of the following would be the <u>most</u> likely situation where asbestos may be encountered?

- ○ a   In an old re-wireable (semi-enclosed) fuseboard.
- ○ b   In a modern grid type ceiling tile.
- ○ c   Within foam based heating pipe insulation.
- ○ d   Within an old type 2 circuit breaker.

Notes

Questions and answers

The questions in Sample test: Unit 301 are repeated below with worked-through answers and comments.

1 The Electricity at Work Regulations is a

- ○ a   statutory document which relates to employees only
- ○ b   non-statutory document which relates to employers only
- ◉ c   statutory document which relates to employers and employees
- ○ d   non-statutory document relating to employers and employees.

Answer c
The Electricity at Work Regulations is a **statutory** (legal) document. Both employers and employees have a duty to comply with this document while at work.

2 To minimise the risk when others are working at height in the same location, the <u>most</u> appropriate item of PPE to be worn would be

- ○ a   a high-visibility jacket
- ○ b   ear defenders
- ◉ c   a hard hat
- ○ d   gloves.

Answer c
The risk when others are working at heights is falling objects. The **most** appropriate form of protection for the whole head is a hard hat.

3 All accidents at work which involve hospitalisation for more than three days must be reported as part of

- ○ a   RODER
- ◉ b   RIDDOR
- ○ c   RIDER
- ○ d   RUDDER.

Answer b
The abbreviation RIDDOR stands for Reporting of Injuries, Disease and Dangerous Occurrences Regulations. Under RIDDOR all accidents which result in:
– death
– loss of limb
– loss of consciousness
– loss of work for more than three days
must be reported to the Health and Safety Executive or the Local Authority Environmental Health office. This is a statutory duty of all employers.

4 If a trainee electrician, while working on a construction site, notices a live conductor which is exposed to touch, the trainee should

○ a   tape it up
◉ b   report it to a supervisor immediately
○ c   short out the ends causing the fuse to blow
○ d   write a report on the incident and post it to the office.

Answer b
As the trainee has noticed the risk, it is that person's duty to report it, straight away, to a person who can safely deal with it. In many circumstances, trying to take action by taping it up or trying to resolve the problem in other ways may lead to further danger to oneself and others. A responsible person, such as a supervisor, would understand the full extent of the risks involved and is therefore in a position to act in the correct way.

5 When a hazard is identified in the workplace, an employee must

○ a   report the hazard at the next safety briefing
○ b   mention it if an accident occurs
◉ c   report it immediately to a supervisor
○ d   write it down and post a report to the office.

Answer c
Any identified hazards must be reported immediately to a supervisor who is in a position to assess the risk. Hazards should not be ignored and there should be no delay in reporting them.

6 The <u>main</u> purpose for having a visitors' book in a workplace is to

- ○ a   provide data to the police on people's movements
- ◉ b   account for all persons in the event of an emergency
- ○ c   keep records in case items are stolen
- ○ d   restrict access to people who have not got hard hats.

Answer b

Whilst visitors' books may be used to monitor those people entering and leaving a workplace for security reasons, the main purpose is to account for all people in that building in the event of emergency evacuation, such as a fire, to ensure that no persons remain in the building.

7 If an electrician discovers an item of PPE is faulty, the item should be returned, for replacement, to the

- ◉ a   electrician's employer
- ○ b   Health and Safety Executive
- ○ c   union representative
- ○ d   customer or one of their representatives.

Answer a

It is essential that faulty items of PPE are returned for replacement immediately. As it is the employer's responsibility to provide PPE, items should be returned to the employer.

8 PPE should be selected for a particular task

- ○ a   as a substitution for minimising any risks
- ◉ b   following actions to reduce the risks
- ○ c   because reducing the risks would be too expensive
- ○ d   as a quick means to avoid reducing the risks.

Answer b

In all cases, following a risk assessment, all measures should be taken to reduce any risk by removing hazards. Only once risk is reduced should PPE be selected to take into consideration any other hazard that cannot be removed. In certain cases, a risk assessment is the only means of minimising risk and PPE should be selected based on this.

9   The <u>main</u> purpose of visors on hard hats, used when drilling, is to

Notes

- ○   a   provide magnified vision
- ○   b   provide noise protection
- ◉   c   protect the eyes from debris
- ○   d   protect eyes from solar radiation.

Answer c

Some hard hats are fitted with visors, used to protect eyes from flying debris created when drilling. These visors will often protect the whole face, as well as the eyes, as some debris may cause abrasions to skin.

10 When passing metal conduit to a colleague who is working on a tower scaffold, correct PPE <u>must</u> include

- ◉   a   gloves, boots and a hard hat
- ○   b   gloves, boots and a face mask
- ○   c   boots, face mask and a hard hat
- ○   d   face mask, hard hat and gloves.

Answer a

When handling metallic conduit, gloves are required to protect hands and, in case of the conduit or any other items falling, hard hats and boots will provide necessary protection. Face masks are not required as the work detailed does not include the risk of breathing in dust, etc.

11 Access by medical crews is an important consideration when selecting the location of a

- ○   a   fire alarm indicator panel
- ○   b   car park
- ○   c   store room
- ◉   d   first aid treatment room.

Answer d

The location of a first aid treatment room should be in a position providing easy access for medical crews. If medical crews have to transport patients across a construction site, or through corridors within a building, the risk of further injury to the patient is increased.

12 Which one of the following arrangements would comply with current safety guidelines when using a ladder as a means of access to the flat roof on a building?

a

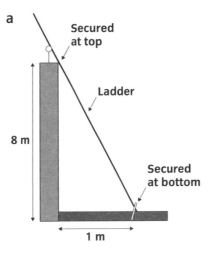

b

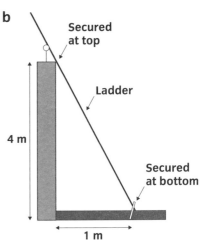

c

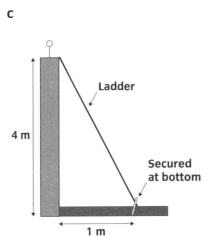

d

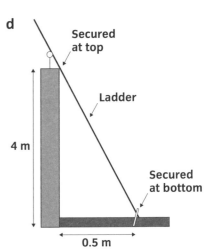

○ a
◉ b
○ c
○ d

Answer b

Diagram b shows the correct arrangement as the ladder extends beyond the climb-off point, it is secured at both the top and bottom, and it provides the correct ratio of height to distance of 4:1. Diagram a shows a height of 8 m to a distance of 1 m from the wall to the ladder base. Diagram c shows the ladder to be too short therefore providing no hold on point when climbing off the ladder. Diagram d shows that the ladder is only 0.5 m distance from the wall even though the height is 4 m.

13 The warning sign shown below indicates a danger of

- ○ a   cable fires
- ◉ b   oxidising chemicals
- ○ c   tunnel fires
- ○ d   exploding chemicals.

Answer b

The diagram shows a standard symbol used by the Chemicals (Hazard Information and Packaging for Supply) Regulations, which indicates that chemicals that react exothermically (oxidising) with other chemicals are contained within the package.

14 Which one of the following is the <u>most</u> likely hazard when drilling 8 mm holes in a plastered wall, 1200 mm above the floor in a domestic dwelling?

- ⦿ a   Drilling into buried cables.
- ○ b   Falling from a height.
- ○ c   Debris falling from above.
- ○ d   Handling chemicals.

Answer a
From the list, the most likely hazard would be drilling into buried cables. As the hole to be drilled is 1200 mm (1.2 m) above level ground with no excavations, this would not be classed as working from heights, or create a risk of falling debris from drilling. As no mention of any chemicals was made in the question, this task would not involve the use of chemicals.

15 Which one of the following would be the <u>most</u> likely situation where asbestos may be encountered?

- ⦿ a   In an old re-wireable (semi-enclosed) fuseboard.
- ○ b   In a modern grid type ceiling tile.
- ○ c   Within foam based heating pipe insulation.
- ○ d   Within an old type 2 circuit breaker.

Answer a
Old semi-enclosed fuses can contain asbestos, which acted as arc containment material. More recent fuses of this type will house the fuse wire in ceramic holders. Care must be taken when removing, working on or disposing of old type fuses where asbestos may be contained. Asbestos is also likely to be present in the holder mounted on the fuseboard as well as the fuse carrier.

Answer key

Sample test: Unit 301

Question	Answer
1	c
2	c
3	b
4	b
5	c
6	b
7	a
8	b
9	c
10	a
11	d
12	b
13	b
14	a
15	a

Notes

Exam practice 2

Exam practice 2

Notes

Sample test: Unit 305

The sample test below has 15 questions, the same number as the online exam, and its structure follows that of the online exam. The test appears first without answers, so you can use it as a mock exam. It is then repeated with worked-through answers and comments. Finally, there is an answer key for easy reference.

Answer the questions by filling in the circle next to your chosen option. You will be allowed to take a clean copy of BS 7671 into the exam with you.

1 **A distribution circuit protected by a 20 A BS 1361 device, when forming part of a 230 V TT installation, <u>must</u> disconnect under earth fault conditions within a maximum time of**

   ○ a   0.2 seconds
   ○ b   0.4 seconds
   ○ c   1 second
   ○ d   5 seconds.

2 **The maximum permitted earth fault loop impedance for a socket-outlet circuit, forming part of a 230 V TN-S system, protected by a 16 A BS 88 device is**

   ○ a   2.70 Ω
   ○ b   3.83 Ω
   ○ c   4.18 Ω
   ○ d   5.11 Ω.

3 **Which one of the following socket-outlet arrangements would <u>not</u> require additional protection by a 30 mA RCD?**

   ○ a   13 A socket-outlets for general use wired in a surface conduit.
   ○ b   13 A socket-outlets wired in surface conduit for a specifically labelled use.
   ○ c   16 A socket-outlets intended to supply mobile equipment to be used outdoors.
   ○ d   16 A socket-outlets in a swimming pool location.

4 Which of the following is <u>not</u> a provision for basic protection against electric shock?

○ a   Barriers.
○ b   Enclosures.
○ c   Electrical separation.
○ d   Insulation of live parts.

5 When considering protection against fire caused by electrical equipment, the spread of fire by burning liquids must be minimised. This applies to equipment which holds a quantity of flammable liquid above

○ a   25 litres
○ b   20 litres
○ c   15 litres
○ d   10 litres.

6 In three-phase a.c. circuits, the conductor designated as L2 shall be coloured

○ a   brown
○ b   blue
○ c   black
○ d   grey.

7 Where an installation incorporates an RCD, a prominent notice shall be fixed at or near the origin of the installation informing persons that the RCD should be tested, using the test button,

○ a   monthly
○ b   quarterly
○ c   half yearly
○ d   annually.

Notes

Notes

8 The diagram shows a buried cable linking two socket-outlets in a domestic dwelling. In order to provide adequate impact protection, this cable should be

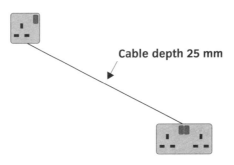

Cable depth 25 mm

- ○ a   protected by a 30 mA RCD
- ○ b   enclosed in earthed metallic conduit
- ○ c   incorporated in PVC conduit
- ○ d   enclosed in PVC insulated trunking.

9 Which one of the following types of connection is required to be accessible for inspection, testing and maintenance?

- ○ a   A compound-filled encapsulating joint.
- ○ b   A joint designed to be buried in the ground.
- ○ c   A 30 A joint box with screwed terminals.
- ○ d   A joint made by welding or appropriate compression.

10 Which one of the following devices is suitable for isolation, emergency switching and functional switching?

- ○ a   Switched fused connection unit to BS 1363.
- ○ b   A 45 A plug and socket-outlet to BS EN 60309.
- ○ c   A 16 A plug and socket-outlet to BS EN 60309.
- ○ d   Un-switched fused connection unit to BS 1363.

11 A firefighter's switch shall be

- ○ a   coloured red with the off position at the bottom
- ○ b   coloured yellow with the off position at the top
- ○ c   coloured yellow with the off position at the bottom
- ○ d   coloured red with the off position at the top.

12 In a location containing a bath or shower, 13 A socket-outlets are prohibited within a distance of 3 m horizontally from the boundary of

Notes

○ a   zone 1
○ b   zone 2
○ c   the plug hole
○ d   a light point.

13 In agricultural installations, measures for protection against fire shall be provided by RCDs having a rated residual operating current not exceeding

○ a   30 mA
○ b   100 mA
○ c   300 mA
○ d   500 mA.

14 Which one of the following circuits does <u>not</u> require additional protection by an RCD when forming part of a temporary installation at a fairground?

○ a   A 230 V lighting circuit within arm's reach.
○ b   A 230 V 16 A socket-outlet circuit.
○ c   A 110 V socket-outlet circuit.
○ d   A 12 V SELV lighting circuit.

15 In order to avoid the overheating of floor or ceiling heating systems, measures shall be applied to limit the zone temperature to a maximum of

○ a   35°C
○ b   80°C
○ c   90°C
○ d   160°C.

Questions and answers

The questions in Sample test: Unit 305 are repeated below with worked-through answers and comments.

1   **A distribution circuit protected by a 20 A BS 1361 device, when forming part of a 230 V TT installation, <u>must</u> disconnect under earth fault conditions within a maximum time of**

○ a   0.2 seconds
○ b   0.4 seconds
◉ c   1 second
○ d   5 seconds.

Answer c

BS 7671, Chapter 41 sets out the requirements for disconnection as part of Automatic Disconnection of Supply (ADS). In particular, Table 41.1 gives disconnection times for all final circuits rated at or under 32 A. However, as the question relates to a distribution circuit forming part of a TT installation, Regulation 411.3.2.4 states that any circuit not included in Table 41.1 or a distribution circuit must disconnect in a time not exceeding 1 second.

2   **The maximum permitted earth fault loop impedance for a socket-outlet circuit, forming part of a 230 V TN-S system, protected by a 16 A BS 88 device is**

◉ a   2.70 Ω
○ b   3.83 Ω
○ c   4.18 Ω
○ d   5.11 Ω.

Answer a

A final circuit, such as a socket-outlet circuit forming part of a 230 V TN-S system must disconnect in 0.4 seconds as stated in BS 7671, Table 41.1. The maximum earth fault loop impedance for this circuit under these conditions is found using Table 41.2 'Maximum earth fault loop impedances (Z_S) for fuses, for 0.4 s disconnection time with U_0 of 230 V'. Under this table, a 16 A, BS 88 device has a maximum impedance of 2.70 Ω.

3   Which one of the following socket-outlet arrangements would <u>not</u> require additional protection by a 30 mA RCD?

○ a   13 A socket-outlets for general use wired in a surface conduit.

◉ b   13 A socket-outlets wired in surface conduit for a specifically labelled use.

○ c   16 A socket-outlets intended to supply mobile equipment to be used outdoors.

○ d   16 A socket-outlets in a swimming pool location.

Answer b

BS 7671, Regulation 411.3.3 states that additional protection by the use of an RCD in accordance with Regulation 415.1 (having a residual current setting no greater than 30 mA) shall be provided for socket-outlets having a rated current not exceeding 20 A (options a and d) or for mobile equipment with a current rating not exceeding 32 A for use outdoors (option c). The regulation continues by stating that a socket-outlet, provided for a specific item of equipment, and labelled to indicate this is allowed as an exception.

Examiner's tip: Be very careful of the negative questions, ie 'Which one of the following is <u>not</u>…' If read too quickly, the 'not' may be overlooked.

4   Which of the following is <u>not</u> a provision for basic protection against electric shock?

○ a   Barriers.

○ b   Enclosures.

◉ c   Electrical separation.

○ d   Insulation of live parts.

Answer c

Electrical separation is a listed protective measure against faults. Basic protection is a means of stopping contact with parts intended to be live and options a, b and d are all listed under BS 7671, Section 416 as provisions for basic protection.

Hint: Sometimes it is easier to find things in BS 7671 by using the contents sections. By using the main contents page, detail regarding electric shock can be found in Chapter 41. Within the contents page for Chapter 41, basic protection is listed as Section 416 where the above listed methods are stated without the need to go to Section 416. Every chapter has a contents page detailing the headings of each section.

Notes

Examiner's tip: Be very careful of the negative questions, ie 'Which one of the following is <u>not</u>…' If read too quickly, the 'not' may be overlooked. In this case, the first option might be seen as the correct answer as it is a provision for basic protection.

5 **When considering protection against fire caused by electrical equipment, the spread of fire by burning liquids must be minimised. This applies to equipment which holds a quantity of flammable liquid above**

- ⦿ a   25 litres
- ○ b   20 litres
- ○ c   15 litres
- ○ d   10 litres.

Answer a

BS 7671, Chapter 42 contains the requirements for protection against fire and thermal effects; in particular, section 421 contains detail for protection against fire caused by electrical equipment. Regulation 421.5 states that adequate precautions shall be made to prevent the spread of any significant quantity of flammable liquid. Note 2 states that a significant quantity of liquid is generally accepted as being above 25 litres.

Hint: Once again, use of the contents page may prove to be a quicker method of finding the required information as there are no listings in the index page under 'liquid' or 'spread', etc. Clues in the question may help in navigation by the contents pages.

Examiner's tip: Make sure you look at any notes that may be present below a regulation or table.

6 **In three-phase a.c. circuits, the conductor designated as L2 shall be coloured**

- ○ a   brown
- ○ b   blue
- ⦿ c   black
- ○ d   grey.

Answer c

BS 7671, Table 51 provides detail regarding identification of conductors in a.c. power circuits. The identification colours of three-phase circuits are

– L1   brown
– N   blue
– L2   black
– L3   grey.

7   **Where an installation incorporates an RCD, a prominent notice shall be fixed at or near the origin of the installation informing persons that the RCD should be tested, using the test button,**

- ○ a   monthly
- ◉ b   quarterly
- ○ c   half yearly
- ○ d   annually.

Answer b

BS 7671, Chapter 51, Section 514 contains information on identification and notices. Regulation 514.12.2 states that an installation containing an RCD shall have a notice fixed at or near the origin of the installation, a sample of which is given. The notice states that the RCD shall be tested quarterly by pressing the button marked 'T' or 'Test'.

Hint: The keyword in this question, which will help you find the answer within BS 7671, is 'notice'.

8   **The diagram shows a buried cable linking two socket-outlets in a domestic dwelling. In order to provide adequate impact protection, this cable should be**

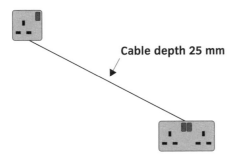

Cable depth 25 mm

- ○ a   protected by a 30 mA RCD
- ◉ b   enclosed in earthed metallic conduit
- ○ c   incorporated in PVC conduit
- ○ d   enclosed in PVC insulated trunking.

Notes

Answer b

BS 7671, Section 522 gives requirements for the selection and erection of wiring systems in relation to external influences. In particular, section 522.6 deals with impact protection. Regulation 522.6.6 states that any cable concealed in a wall at a depth of less than 50 mm shall meet one of the following criteria:

(i)   incorporate an earthed metallic covering (eg SWA)
(ii)   be enclosed in earthed conduit
(iii)   be enclosed in earthed trunking or ducting
(iv)   be mechanically protected to prevent the penetration by nails etc
(v)   be installed in the zone of protection.

As the route of the cable in the diagram does not fall into the zone of protection, the only alternative left is to enclose in earthed conduit. As PVC conduit or trunking cannot be earthed, nor does it provide adequate protection against nails or screws etc, the answer must be option b. If the cable was run in the zone of protection as described in regulation 522.6.6 item (v), then the cable must have additional protection by an RCD as stated in regulation 522.6.7 where the installation is not under effective supervision by skilled or instructed persons. As the installation is a domestic dwelling, skilled or instructed persons would not be supervising this installation.

Hint: The protection by 30 mA RCD is an 'additional protection' requirement where the cable is installed in the zone of protection and therefore is not acceptable as the only means of protection against impact.

9   **Which one of the following types of connection is required to be accessible for inspection, testing and maintenance?**

○ a   A compound-filled encapsulating joint.
○ b   A joint designed to be buried in the ground.
◉ c   A 30 A joint box with screwed terminals.
○ d   A joint made by welding or appropriate compression.

Answer c

BS 7671, Section 526 details requirements for electrical connections. Regulation 526.3 states that every connection must be accessible for inspection, testing and maintenance except for:

(i)   A joint designed to be buried in the ground

(ii)   A compound-filled or encapsulated joint

(iii)   A connection between a cold tail and the heating element as in ceiling, floor or trace heating

(iv)   A joint made by welding, soldering, brazing or appropriate compression

(v)   A joint forming part of equipment complying with appropriate product standards.

From the above, it is clear that a joint box involving screw type terminals must be accessible.

10 Which one of the following devices is suitable for isolation, emergency switching and functional switching?

- ⦿ a   Switched fused connection unit to BS 1363.
- ○ b   A 45 A plug and socket-outlet to BS EN 60309.
- ○ c   A 16 A plug and socket-outlet to BS EN 60309.
- ○ d   Un-switched fused connection unit to BS 1363.

Answer a

BS 7671, Section 537 gives requirements for isolation and switching. Table 53.2 gives guidance on the selection of protective, isolation and switching devices. The options are not suitable for isolation, emergency switching and functional switching, with the exception of the switched, fused connection unit.

11 A firefighter's switch shall be

- ○ a   coloured red with the off position at the bottom
- ○ b   coloured yellow with the off position at the top
- ○ c   coloured yellow with the off position at the bottom
- ⦿ d   coloured red with the off position at the top.

Answer d

The requirements for firefighter's switches are detailed in BS 7671, Section 537.6 and in particular, Regulation 537.6.4 (see index or contents) where items (i) and (ii) state that the switch must be coloured red (i) with the off position at the top (ii).

12 In a location containing a bath or shower, 13 A socket-outlets are prohibited within a distance of 3 m horizontally from the boundary of

◉ a   zone 1
○ b   zone 2
○ c   the plug hole
○ d   a light point.

Answer a

A location containing a bath or shower is classified as a special location, which is detailed in BS 7671, Part 7, Section 701. Regulation 701.512.3 gives requirements for the erection of switchgear, controlgear and accessories in relation to the zones within this type of location.

13 In agricultural installations, measures for protection against fire shall be provided by RCDs having a rated residual operating current not exceeding

○ a   30 mA
○ b   100 mA
◉ c   300 mA
○ d   500 mA.

Answer c

Agricultural installations are classified as special locations as detailed in BS 7671, Part 7, Section 705. Protection against thermal effects are detailed in Regulation 705.422.7, which states that protection shall be provided by an RCD having a rated residual operating current not exceeding 300 mA.

14 Which one of the following circuits does <u>not</u> require additional protection by an RCD when forming part of a temporary installation at a fairground?

○ a   A 230 V lighting circuit within arm's reach.
○ b   A 230 V 16 A socket-outlet circuit.
○ c   A 110 V socket-outlet circuit.
◉ d   A 12 V SELV lighting circuit.

Answer d

Temporary installations at fairgrounds are covered by the requirements of BS 7671, Part 7, Section 740. Regulation 740.415.1 gives requirements for additional protection by RCDs and states that RCDs in accordance with 405.1.1 shall protect circuits for

(i)   lighting
(ii) socket-outlets rated up to 32 A
(iii) mobile equipment connected by flexible cable with a current-carrying capacity up to 32 A.

The regulation continues stating that the requirements do not apply to
(i)   circuits protected by SELV.

Hint: As in many questions, clues as to the location of the answer in BS 7671 can be found in the question.

Examiner's tip: Be careful of negative questions.

15 In order to avoid the overheating of floor or ceiling heating systems, measures shall be applied to limit the zone temperature to a maximum of

- a   35°C
- b   80°C
- c   90°C
- d   160°C.

Answer b

The specific requirements for floor and ceiling heating systems are given in BS 7671, Part 7, Section 753. Regulation 753.424.1.1 gives specific requirements for limiting the temperature of the zone where heating units are installed to a maximum temperature of 80°C.

Answer key

Sample test: Unit 305

Question	Answer
1	c
2	a
3	b
4	c
5	a
6	c
7	b
8	b
9	c
10	a
11	d
12	a
13	c
14	d
15	b

Exam practice 3

Exam practice 3

Sample test: Unit 309

The sample test below has 30 questions, the same number as the online exam, and its structure follows that of the online exam. The test appears first without answers, so you can use it as a mock exam. It is then repeated with worked-through answers and comments. Finally, there is an answer key for easy reference.

Answer the questions by filling in the circle next to your chosen option.

1 voltage drop $= \dfrac{length \times I_b \times mV/A/m}{1000}$

Using the formula shown above, the correct transposition in order to determine the circuit length is

○ a $\dfrac{1000 \times I_b \times mV/A/m}{voltage\ drop}$

○ b $\dfrac{voltage\ drop \times I_b \times 1000}{mV/A/m}$

○ c $\dfrac{voltage\ drop \times 1000}{I_b \times mV/A/m}$

○ d $\dfrac{1000 \times I_b}{mV/A/m \times voltage\ drop}$

2 For the triangle shown below, the length of the hypotenuse marked 'h' is

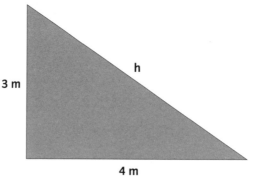

○ a   3 m
○ b   5 m
○ c   12 m
○ d   25 m.

3 If a room measured 12 m by 6 m, the floor area would be

○ a $36\,m^2$
○ b $36\,m^3$
○ c $72\,m^2$
○ d $72\,m^3$.

4 The derived SI unit of measurement of velocity is

○ a   miles per hour
○ b   light-years
○ c   metres per hour
○ d   metres per second.

5 Inductive reactance is measured in

○ a   watts
○ b   joules
○ c   ohms
○ d   henrys.

6 Impedance in a.c. circuits can be determined by the formula

○ a $X - R$
○ b $\sqrt{X + R}$
○ c $X + R$
○ d $\sqrt{R^2 + X^2}$

7 The power factor of a circuit can be determined using a

○ a   wattmeter, voltmeter and ammeter
○ b   voltmeter, ammeter and ohmmeter
○ c   ammeter, ohmmeter and wattmeter
○ d   ohmmeter, wattmeter and voltmeter.

Notes

8 **When measuring the current flow through a small powered d.c. component, an ammeter may be used if connected**

○ a   in parallel to the component
○ b   in series to the component
○ c   to a voltage transformer
○ d   to a current transformer.

9 **A mass, when at sea level, will have a weight equal to**

○ a $\dfrac{mass}{gravity}$

○ b $mass^2 \times gravity$

○ c $mass \times gravity$

○ d $\dfrac{gravity}{mass}$

10 **For the weights to be balanced as shown in the diagram below, the distance marked 'X' must be**

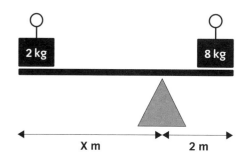

○ a   8 m
○ b   10 m
○ c   16 m
○ d   20 m.

11 The force to be applied in order to raise the 500 kg mass is approximately

Force

500 kg

- ○ a   125 N
- ○ b   1250 N
- ○ c   5000 N
- ○ d   20 000 N.

12 Stored energy is called

- ○ a   potential energy
- ○ b   positive energy
- ○ c   preserved energy
- ○ d   portable energy.

13 Due to losses, the efficiency of a gear system will require a

- ○ a   greater input power to output power
- ○ b   smaller input power to output power
- ○ c   capacitor for power factor correction
- ○ d   inductor for power factor correction.

14 In order to raise a 200 kg mass a distance of 10 m in 20 seconds, the mechanical power needed is approximately

- a 9.81 watts
- b 98.1 watts
- c 981 watts
- d 9.81 kilowatts.

15 If a machine gear system has an input mechanical power of 4.5 kW and an output power of 3.8 kW, its efficiency is

- a 0.84%
- b 16.56%
- c 68.87%
- d 84.44%.

16 Current is described as a flow of

- a neutrons
- b protons
- c electrons
- d photons.

17 Which one of the following materials is classed as a conductor?

- a Carbon.
- b Mica.
- c Butyl.
- d PVC.

18 If an insulator between two conductors had a measured resistance value of 150 MΩ and a voltage was applied between the conductors of 750 V, the current flow would be

- a 5 µA
- b 2 mA
- c 0.2 A
- d 5 A.

19 A composite cable is one that has

- a   bare conductors
- b   one layer of insulation only
- c   a layer of insulation and a sheath
- d   screening between the conductor and insulation.

20 If copper has a resistivity of 0.0178 μΩ/m, a copper conductor having a csa of 2.5 mm^2 and a length of 120 m would have a resistance, at 20°C, of

- a   0.37 mΩ
- b   0.85 Ω
- c   8.51 Ω
- d   2.69 kΩ.

21 If a copper conductor had a measured resistance of 0.445 Ω at 20°C and a length of 100 m, given that the resistivity of copper is 0.0178 μΩ/m, the csa of the conductor would be

- a   4 mm^2
- b   6 mm^2
- c   10 mm^2
- d   16 mm^2.

22 If the resistance of a circuit increases by a small amount and the voltage remains constant, the value of current will

- a   be zero
- b   increase
- c   decrease
- d   remain constant.

23 If a resistor connected to a 200 V d.c. supply caused a current flow of 20 μA, the value of resistance is

- a   10 μΩ
- b   10 mΩ
- c   10 kΩ
- d   10 MΩ.

24 The circuit current (Is) for the circuit shown in the diagram below would be

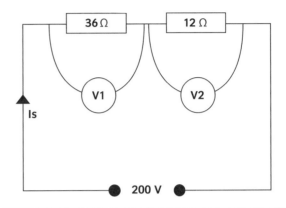

- ○ a 4.16 A
- ○ b 12.82 A
- ○ c 16.68 A
- ○ d 22.22 A.

25 For the circuit shown in the diagram below, the voltage meter (V2) would indicate a voltage measurement of

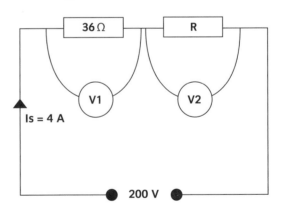

- ○ a 36 V
- ○ b 50 V
- ○ c 56 V
- ○ d 144 V.

26 **For the circuit shown in the diagram below, the circuit current (Is) would be**

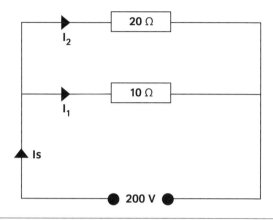

- a   6.67 A
- b   30 A
- c   667 A
- d   1333 A.

27 **The value of current through each resistor is**

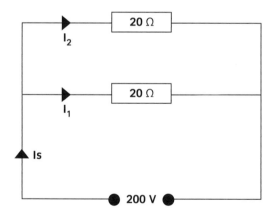

- a   5 A
- b   10 A
- c   20 A
- d   50 A.

Notes

28 In a circuit that has a total resistance of 100 Ω and a circuit current of 5 A, the total power dissipated is

- ○ a 500 W
- ○ b 2.5 kW
- ○ c 5.0 kW
- ○ d 50 kW.

29 A circuit line and neutral conductor had a total resistance of 1.6 Ω at normal operating temperatures and a load drawing a current of 10 A. The total voltage drop across the circuit would be

- ○ a 0.8 V
- ○ b 1.6 V
- ○ c 8.0 V
- ○ d 16 V.

30 When current flow is increased through a conductor, the effect this will have is to

- ○ a increase temperature which will increase resistance
- ○ b increase temperature which will decrease resistance
- ○ c decrease temperature which will increase resistance
- ○ d decrease temperature which will decrease current.

Questions and answers

The questions in Sample test: Unit 309 are repeated below with worked-through answers and comments.

1   voltage drop $= \dfrac{length \times I_b \times mV/A/m}{1000}$

Using the formula shown above, the correct transposition in order to determine the circuit length is

○ a $\dfrac{1000 \times I_b \times mV/A/m}{voltage\ drop}$

○ b $\dfrac{voltage\ drop \times I_b \times 1000}{mV/A/m}$

◉ c $\dfrac{voltage\ drop \times 1000}{I_b \times mV/A/m}$

○ d $\dfrac{1000 \times I_b}{mV/A/m \times voltage\ drop}$

Answer c

In order to successfully transpose a formula, the following rules must be applied if the formula involves multiplication and division.

1   Any value moved over the '=' sign moves from bottom to top, or top to bottom.
2   Any values that need to be determined must be on their own on one side of the '=' sign.
3   The value to be found must be at the top. Any value that is neither top nor bottom is regarded as top.

So, applying those rules and looking at the formula in the question, the value 'length' is at the top. To get it on its own, the other values beside and below it must be moved over the '=' sign. Remember, voltage drop is not bottom or top so it is regarded as being top. Therefore, I_b and mV/A/m move over to the bottom, and 1000 moves over to the top to get:

$\dfrac{voltage\ drop \times 1000}{I_b \times mV/A/m} = length$

Notes

2 **For the triangle shown below, the length of the hypotenuse marked 'h' is**

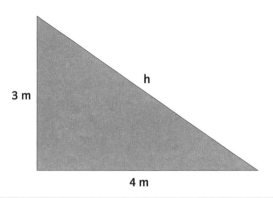

3 m

h

4 m

- ○ a   3 m
- ◉ b   5 m
- ○ c   12 m
- ○ d   25 m.

Answer b

For a right-angled triangle, such as this, Pythagoras's theorem states that the length of the hypotenuse squared is equal to the length of side 'a' squared added to the length of side 'b' squared, therefore:

$$\sqrt{a^2 + b^2} = h$$

so

$$\sqrt{3^2 + 4^2} = 5$$

3 **If a room measured 12 m by 6 m, the floor area would be**

- ○ a   36 m^2
- ○ b   36 m^3
- ◉ c   72 m^2
- ○ d   72 m^3.

Answer c

Area is found by multiplying the two sides together, therefore:

$$12 \times 6 = 72$$

Since area is measured in metres square (m^2), the answer is 72 m^2.

4   The derived SI unit of measurement of velocity is

- ○ a   miles per hour
- ○ b   light-years
- ○ c   metres per hour
- ⦿ d   metres per second.

Answer d

The base SI units for distance and time respectively are metres and seconds. To measure distance over time (velocity) the derived unit would be metres per second.

5   Inductive reactance is measured in

- ○ a   watts
- ○ b   joules
- ⦿ c   ohms
- ○ d   henrys.

Answer c

The unit of measurement is ohms as the reactance acts as a form of resistance in a circuit and when both reactance and resistance are present in an a.c. circuit, the product is impedance.

6   Impedance in a.c. circuits can be determined by the formula

- ○ a $X - R$
- ○ b $\sqrt{X + R}$
- ○ c $X + R$
- ⦿ d $\sqrt{R^2 + X^2}$

Notes

Answer d

As with determining the hypotenuse of a triangle using Pythagoras's theorem, the impedance of a circuit is found in the same way, by using the reactance of the circuit together with the resistance.

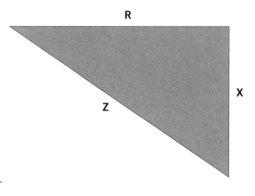

So $Z = \sqrt{R^2 + x^2}$

7 The power factor of a circuit can be determined using a

- ⦿ a   wattmeter, voltmeter and ammeter
- ◯ b   voltmeter, ammeter and ohmmeter
- ◯ c   ammeter, ohmmeter and wattmeter
- ◯ d   ohmmeter, wattmeter and voltmeter.

Answer a

$$pf = \frac{kW}{kVA} \text{ or } \frac{W}{VA}$$

Therefore by measuring the voltage and current of the circuit, applied to the wattage, the value of power factor may be found.

8 When measuring the current flow through a small powered d.c. component, an ammeter may be used if connected

- ◯ a   in parallel to the component
- ⦿ b   in series to the component
- ◯ c   to a voltage transformer
- ◯ d   to a current transformer.

Answer b

Current flows around a circuit; therefore, in order to measure the current, the ammeter must be connected in series with the load. Voltage or current transformers will not work as transformers require a.c. An instrument connected in parallel to the load will often be used to measure potential difference (voltage).

9   A mass, when at sea level, will have a weight equal to

○ a $\dfrac{mass}{gravity}$

○ b $mass^2 \times gravity$

◉ c $mass \times gravity$

○ d $\dfrac{gravity}{mass}$

Answer c

Mass is the same whether in space or on earth at sea level. Weight is found by applying the force of gravity to the mass (9.81 N), therefore:

$weight = mass \times gravity$

10 **For the weights to be balanced as shown in the diagram below, the distance marked 'X' must be**

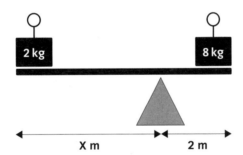

◉ a   8 m

○ b   10 m

○ c   16 m

○ d   20 m.

Answer a

By using the formula for force:

$force(1) \times distance(1) = force(2) \times distance(2)$

we can transpose to

$\dfrac{force(2) \times distance(2)}{force(1)} = distance(1)$

therefore

$\dfrac{8 \times 2}{2} = 8\,m$

Notes

11 **The force to be applied in order to raise the 500 kg mass is approximately**

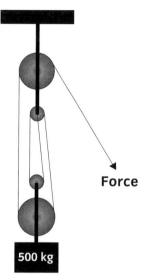

Force

500 kg

○ a   125 N
◉ b   1250 N
○ c   5000 N
○ d   20 000 N.

Answer b

The first consideration is converting the mass to a downward force acting against the pulley block. This is done by applying the force of gravity which is 9.81 N (approximately 10 N). Therefore:

force = mass × gravity

so

force = 500 × 10 = 5000 N

A pulley system having four ropes on the block (excluding the pulling rope) has an advantage of 4:1, therefore:

$$\frac{5000\ N}{4} = 1250\ N$$

12 Stored energy is called

- ⊙ a   potential energy
- ○ b   positive energy
- ○ c   preserved energy
- ○ d   portable energy.

Answer a
Where energy is stored, for example a coiled spring, the energy is known as potential energy.

13 Due to losses, the efficiency of a gear system will require a

- ⊙ a   greater input power to output power
- ○ b   smaller input power to output power
- ○ c   capacitor for power factor correction
- ○ d   inductor for power factor correction.

Answer a
Due to losses in a gear system, such as friction, heat or noise is produced. These cause consumption in energy and as a result, more power is required to be put into the gear system (input) than is delivered by the system (output). Power factor correction has nothing to do with the efficiency of a gear system.

14 In order to raise a 200 kg mass a distance of 10 m in 20 seconds, the mechanical power needed is approximately

- ○ a   9.81 watts
- ○ b   98.1 watts
- ⊙ c   981 watts
- ○ d   9.81 kilowatts.

Answer c
By using the formula:

$$\text{power} = \frac{mass \times gravity \times distance}{time}$$

we can calculate the power required so:

$$\frac{200 \times 9.81 \times 10}{20} = 981 \text{ watts}$$

15 If a machine gear system has an input mechanical power of 4.5 kW and an output power of 3.8 kW, its efficiency is

- ○ a   0.84%
- ○ b   16.56%
- ○ c   68.87%
- ◉ d   84.44%.

Answer d

The efficiency of a machine or gear system is found by

$$\% = \frac{output \times 100}{input}$$

therefore

$$\frac{3.8 \times 100}{4.5} = 84.44\%$$

16 Current is described as a flow of

- ○ a   neutrons
- ○ b   protons
- ◉ c   electrons
- ○ d   photons.

Answer c

Current flowing in a circuit is the flow of electrons from one atom to another within the cable. The measure of the flow of electrons is charge (coulombs) and the amount of charge in a time period is current flow in amperes. When a number of electrons flow through a section of cable in one second, one ampere flows. That number of electrons is

$$6.3 \times 10^{18} = 1 \text{ coulomb}$$

which is equal to

6300000000000000000 electrons.

17 Which one of the following materials is classed as a conductor?

◉ a   Carbon.
○ b   Mica.
○ c   Butyl.
○ d   PVC.

Answer a
PVC, mica and butyl are all classed as insulators. However, carbon is often used as a conducting material, such as for motor brushes.

18 If an insulator between two conductors had a measured resistance value of 150 MΩ and a voltage was applied between the conductors of 750 V, the current flow would be

◉ a   5 μA
○ b   2 mA
○ c   0.2 A
○ d   5 A.

Answer a
Using Ohm's Law, and ensuring the correct indices are used for MΩ ($\times 10^6$), the correct calculation is:

$$\frac{750\,V}{150 \times 10^6\,\Omega} = 5 \times 10^{-6} = 5\mu A$$

19 A composite cable is one that has

○ a   bare conductors
○ b   one layer of insulation only
◉ c   a layer of insulation and a sheath
○ d   screening between the conductor and insulation.

Answer c
Composite cables have sheathing around the conductors and insulation.

20 If copper has a resistivity of 0.0178 μΩ/m, a copper conductor having a csa of 2.5 mm² and a length of 120 m would have a resistance, at 20°C, of

○ a   0.37 mΩ
◉ b   0.85 Ω
○ c   8.51 Ω
○ d   2.69 kΩ.

Notes

Answer b

Using the resistivity formula below, we can calculate the resistance.

$$R = \frac{\rho L}{A} \text{ at } 20°C$$

Hint: It is worth noting that all of the indices in this formula cancel each other out, therefore:

$$\frac{0.0178 \times 10^{-6} \, \Omega \times 120 \, m}{2.5 \times 10^{-6}}$$

Remember, mm are x10^{-3} but mm^2 are x10^{-6}. This becomes

$$\frac{0.0178 \, \Omega \times 120 \, m}{2.5} = 0.85 \, \Omega$$

---

21 **If a copper conductor had a measured resistance of 0.445 Ω at 20°C and a length of 100 m, given that the resistivity of copper is 0.0178 μΩ/m, the csa of the conductor would be**

- ⦿ a   4 mm^2
- ◯ b   6 mm^2
- ◯ c   10 mm^2
- ◯ d   16 mm^2.

Answer a

If you transpose the formula

$$R = \frac{\rho L}{A} \text{ at } 20°C$$

to

$$A = \frac{\rho L}{R} \, mm^2$$

then

$$A = \frac{0.0178 \times 100}{0.445} = 4 \, mm^2$$

22 If the resistance of a circuit increases by a small amount and the voltage remains constant, the value of current will

Notes

- ○ a   be zero
- ◉ c   decrease
- ○ b   increase
- ○ d   remain constant.

Answer c

Ohm's Law shows that a rise in resistance will cause a decrease in current as long as the voltage remains constant, eg

$$\frac{100\,V}{10\,\Omega} = 10\,A$$

and

$$\frac{100\,V}{12\,\Omega} = 8.33\,A$$

so the current decreases.

23 If a resistor connected to a 200 V d.c. supply caused a current flow of 20 µA, the value of resistance is

- ○ a   10 µΩ
- ○ b   10 mΩ
- ○ c   10 kΩ
- ◉ d   10 MΩ.

Answer d

For this calculation of Ohm's Law we must use indices, therefore

$$\frac{200\,V}{20 \times 10^{-6}} = 10 \times 10^{6} = 10\,M\Omega$$

Examiner's tip: If the display in your calculator has a small number in the right hand corner, it means that the value is x10 to the power of (the number displayed in the corner). To convert that number to a more understandable value, push the ENG button, or SHIFT ENG and watch the display, together with the 'power to' number change. When that 'power to' number reaches zero, it is the 'actual value' being displayed.

24 **The circuit current (Is) for the circuit shown in the diagram below, would be**

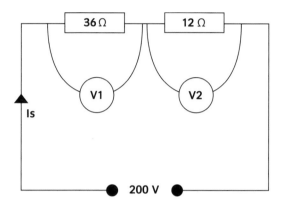

- ⊙ a   4.16 A
- ○ b   12.82 A
- ○ c   16.68 A
- ○ d   22.22 A.

Answer a

Resistors in series are added together to determine the total resistance so the total resistance can be found by

$$36\,\Omega + 12\,\Omega = 48\,\Omega$$

From this we apply Ohm's Law, as follows:

$$I = \frac{200\,V}{48\,\Omega} = 4.16\,A$$

25 For the circuit shown in the diagram below, the voltage meter (V2) **Notes**
would indicate a voltage measurement of

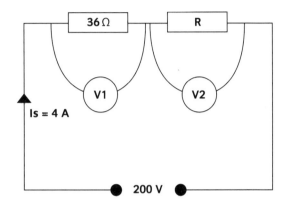

- a   36 V
- b   50 V
- c   56 V
- d   144 V.

Answer c

This can be determined in two ways:

1   Determine the voltage V1 by

$$V1 = 36\,\Omega \times 4\,A = 144\,V$$

then

$$V2 = 200\,V - 144\,V = 56\,V$$

2   $R\,total = \dfrac{200\,V}{4\,A} = 50\,\Omega$

then

$$R = 50\,\Omega - 36\,\Omega = 14\,\Omega$$

and

$$V1 = 14\,\Omega \times 4\,A = 56\,V$$

Notes

26 For the circuit shown in the diagram below, the circuit current (Is) would be

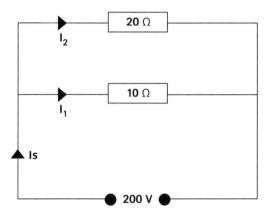

- a   6.67 A
- b   30 A
- c   667 A
- d   1333 A.

Answer b

To determine the circuit current, the total resistance must first be found. This is found by the following formula:

$$\frac{1}{Rt} = \frac{1}{R1} + \frac{1}{R2} \quad \dots \quad \dots$$

so the total resistance is

$$\frac{1}{20} + \frac{1}{10} = \frac{1}{0.15} = 6.667 \ \Omega$$

To determine the current, apply Ohm's Law

$$Is = \frac{200 \text{ V}}{6.667 \ \Omega} = 30 \text{ A}$$

Examiner's tip: To work out the formula for total resistance using a scientific calculator, find the button marked $\boxed{X^1}$ or $\boxed{1/X}$.

To perform the formula above enter the following:

$\boxed{20}\ \boxed{X^1}\ \boxed{+}\ \boxed{10}\ \boxed{X^1}\ \boxed{=}\ \boxed{X^1}\ \boxed{=}$

Always ensure that the last $\boxed{X^1}$ button is pushed.

27 The value of current through each resistor is

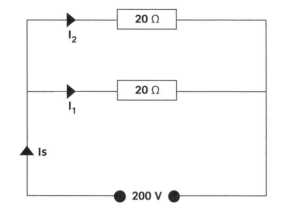

- ○ a   5 A
- ⦿ b   10 A
- ○ c   20 A
- ○ d   50 A.

Answer b

The value of current through each resistor in a parallel circuit can simply be found by applying Ohm's Law to that section of the circuit. Remember, the supply voltage remains constant.

$$\text{Is} = \frac{200\,V}{20\,\Omega} = 10\,A$$

28 In a circuit that has a total resistance of 100 Ω and a circuit current of 5 A, the total power dissipated is

- ○ a   500 W
- ⦿ b   2.5 kW
- ○ c   5.0 kW
- ○ d   50 kW.

Answer b

Power dissipated in a circuit can be determined using the formula

$$P = I^2R$$

so

$$P = 5^2\,A \times 100\,\Omega = 2500\,W \text{ or } 2.5\,kW$$

29 A circuit line and neutral conductor had a total resistance of 1.6 Ω at normal operating temperatures and a load drawing a current of 10 A. The total voltage drop across the circuit would be

- ○ a   0.8 V
- ○ b   1.6 V
- ○ c   8.0 V
- ◉ d   16 V.

Answer d

Voltage dropped across the conductors in the circuit can be determined by applying Ohm's Law using the conductor resistance and load current. The voltage dropped is found by

$$V = 1.6\,\Omega \times 10\,A = 16\,V$$

30 When current flow is increased through a conductor, the effect this will have is to

- ◉ a   increase temperature which will increase resistance
- ○ b   increase temperature which will decrease resistance
- ○ c   decrease temperature which will increase resistance
- ○ d   decrease temperature which will decrease current.

Answer a

Passing current through a conductor will cause the temperature of the conductor to increase; this in turn will cause the resistance of the conductor to also increase.

Answer key

Sample test: Unit 309

Question	Answer	Question	Answer
1	c	16	c
2	b	17	a
3	c	18	a
4	d	19	c
5	c	20	b
6	d	21	a
7	a	22	c
8	b	23	d
9	c	24	a
10	a	25	c
11	b	26	b
12	a	27	b
13	a	28	b
14	c	29	d
15	d	30	a

Notes

Exam practice 4

Exam practice 4

Sample test: Unit 309 Short answer paper

The sample test below has 30 questions, the same number as the written exam, and its structure follows that of the written paper. The test appears first without answers, so you can use it as a mock exam. It is then repeated with worked-through answers and comments.

Answer the questions on some blank sheets of paper and try to time yourself.

1   The direction of the compass needle shown in the diagram below is as a result of the current flow in the coil. Re-draw the diagram showing the direction of the current through the coil.

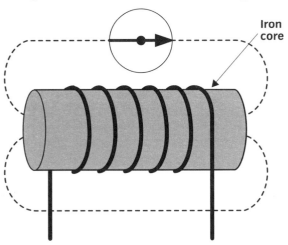

2   A circuit consists of a 2 V cell, a switch and a coil. Draw the circuit and indicate where instruments would be used to measure
    a) electromotive force
    b) electromagnetism.

3   The peak value of a sine wave is 400 V. Calculate the
    a) rms value
    b) average value over a half cycle
    c) peak to peak value.

4   Using a simple block diagram, show how gas, as an energy source, is used to produce electricity.

Notes

5 State **three** reasons for using high voltage a.c. for long distance transmission.

6 Describe briefly how electricity is produced from wind energy.

7 Show, with the aid of a diagram, how **each** of the following loads may be connected to a 400 V, four-wire supply.
   a) 230 V single-phase load.
   b) 400 V three-phase and neutral load.
   c) 400 V three-phase balanced load.

8 Describe briefly the operating principle of a single-phase, double-wound transformer.

9 Show, with the aid of a drawing, the layout of a three-phase Shell type transformer including the position of the primary and secondary windings.

10 A 20:1 step-down transformer is supplied at 230 V a.c. and has a secondary current of 40 A. Calculate the
   a) secondary voltage
   b) primary current
   c) transformer kVA rating.

11 An a.c. circuit consists of a coil having 30 Ω inductive reactance, a 50 Ω resistor, with a capacitor of 20 Ω capacitive reactance connected in series to a 200 V supply. Calculate the circuit current.

12 A circuit consists of a capacitor connected in series with a resistor. Draw an impedance triangle indicating the sides of the triangle representing resistance, capacitive reactance and impedance.

13 Explain what is meant by the terms
   a) true power
   b) apparent power
   c) reactive power.

14 State **three** possible advantages of balancing loads across a three-phase four-wire system.

15 A load of 2.5 kW connected to a 230 V single-phase supply draws a current of 12 A. Calculate the power factor of the load.

Notes

16 a) At which of the points marked A, B, C, D and E, shown in the diagram below, can power factor correction be applied for
    i) individual items of equipment
    ii) the complete installation.

   b) State the component that would be used to correct power factor in a) i) above.

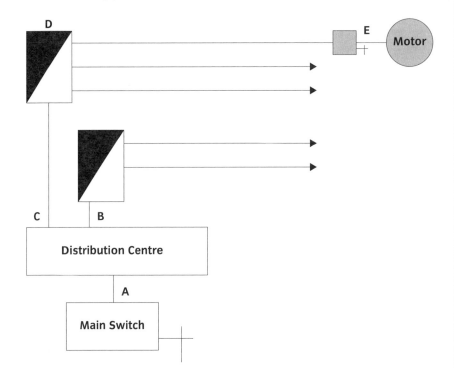

17 Determine, using a phasor diagram to scale, the neutral current for the following three-phase system at unity power factor
    – L1   40 A
    – L2   30 A
    – L3   20 A.

Notes

18 Calculate, using the diagram shown below, the values of the
   a) line voltage of the transformer
   b) load phase current.

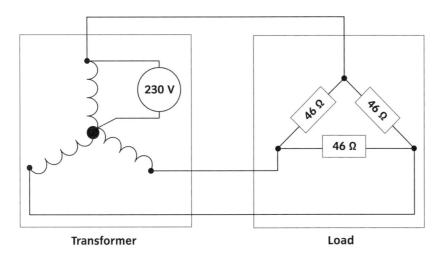

   Transformer   **Load**

19 Draw a fully labelled circuit diagram for a d.c. shunt motor.

20 Explain how starting is achieved in a capacitor start,
   single-phase motor.

21 State **one** application for **each** of the following motors.
   a) Three-phase induction motor.
   b) Single-phase, capacitor start induction motor.
   c) Single-phase universal motor.

22 State **one** suitable starting arrangement for **each** of the
   following motors.
   a) 3 kW single-phase induction motor.
   b) 25 kW three-phase induction motor.
   c) 20 kW three-phase, wound rotor induction motor.

23 Describe the operation of a DOL starter, controlling a small
   milling machine, when the supply voltage to the starter is
   briefly interrupted.

24 Explain which component parts cause the operation of a 6A, 30 mA
   RCBO, protecting a circuit when a
   a) current of 30 mA flows to earth in the circuit
   b) short circuit current flows in the circuit.

25 The illuminance on a surface 4 m directly below a lamp is 200 lux. Determine the level of illuminance on the surface if the lamp is moved 2 metres closer to the surface.

26 a) Explain why compact fluorescent lamps may be selected in preference to GLS lamps.
   b) State **one** disadvantage of using low pressure sodium vapour lamps.

27 Describe, with the aid of a diagram, how the process of convection is used to heat a room using a wall-mounted electric heater.

28 Explain the function of the following components when used in heating systems.
   a) Time switch.
   b) Frost thermostat (frost-stat).
   c) Contactor.

29 State the function of a
   a) thermistor in a domestic heating control system
   b) thermistor in a motor winding
   c) photodiode in a passive infra-red detector.

30 State **one** typical electronic application for **each** of the following components.
   a) Diode.
   b) Triac.
   c) Thyristor.

Questions and answers

The questions in Sample test: Unit 309 Short answer paper are repeated below with worked-through answers and comments.

1 The direction of the compass needle shown in the diagram below is as a result of the current flow in the coil. Re-draw the diagram showing the direction of the current through the coil.

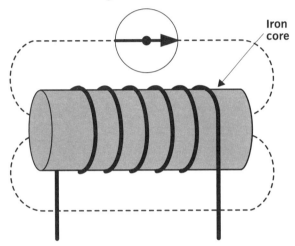

Answer

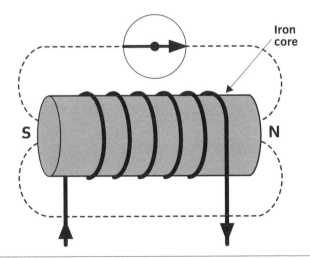

Comments

You need to understand that when a current flows through a conductor, a magnetic field circulates around the conductor (corkscrew or right hand rule). When formed into a coil, the magnetic field forms a north and south pole.

Notes

2 A circuit consists of a 2 V cell, a switch and a coil. Draw the circuit and indicate where instruments would be used to measure
a) electromotive force
b) electromagnetism.

Answer

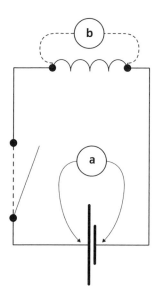

a) Internal to the cell **or** when the cell is off load (switch open).
b) Around the coil (switch closed).

Comments

The voltage of a cell is normally expressed as the voltage (U) on load. The emf (E) of the cell is the open circuit potential. When a current flows in the circuit the internal voltage drop in the cell means that the terminal voltage is less than the internal emf.

$U = E - (I \times R_C)$ *where R_C is resistance of the cell.*

The same rules apply to generators.
The magnetic field will be around the coil.

3   The peak value of a sine wave is 400 V. Calculate the
   a)   rms value
   b)   average value over a half cycle
   c)   peak to peak value.

Answer
   a) $400 \times 0.707 = 282.8$ V
   b) $400 \times 0.63 = 254.4$ V
   c) $2 \times$ peak value $= 800$ V

Comments
This type of question uses a pure sinusoidal (sine) wave only. The peak value is the same as the maximum value of a half cycle of the wave.

The root mean square (rms) value is that value of an a.c. wave that will produce the same heating effect as a d.c. voltage. So 230 V rms a.c. will produce the same heating effect as 230 V d.c. Alternating current supplies are always quoted in rms values. For a standard sine wave the rms value is always 0.707 x peak or maximum value.

The average value is perhaps of less interest to electricians. The average value of a full, 360° sine wave is zero as there is as much above the horizontal line as below. For a half wave the average value is 0.636 × peak value.

The peak to peak value is the vertical measurement from the peak of the positive half wave to the peak of the negative half wave. Assuming both half waves are equal:

peak to peak $= 2 \times$ *peak value*

Notes

4   Using a simple block diagram, show how gas, as an energy source, is used to produce electricity.

Answer

Below is an exemplar diagram showing gas/fire (heat) water/steam/ turbine/a.c. generator.

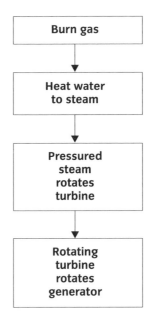

Comments

Gas is used as an energy source and is used to produce heat. The heat turns water to steam to drive the turbine. The turbine is connected to an a.c. generator, which produces electricity up to 25 kV.

5   State **three** reasons for using high voltage a.c. for long distance transmission.

Answer

The higher the voltage for a given power consumption, the less current flows. This
- allows smaller csa cables to be used
- reduces the weight carried by pylons
- reduces power loss.

Comments

The higher the voltage used for a given power, the less current flows.

$(Power = V \times 1)$

The power loss in the cable is proportional to

$I^2 \times R$

and so the system power loss is reduced.

6   Describe briefly how electricity is produced from wind energy.

Answer

A wind turbine, normally a three-bladed propeller or rotor, has the blade shaft connected to a generator, often through a gear box. The rotation of the generator produces electricity.

Comments

There are several different types of wind generator; some have vertical shafts where the generator is mounted below the blades or horizontal types where the generator is mounted behind the blades, often via a gearbox. The basic idea is that the wind blows against the blades, which rotate. These in turn create the rotation of the generator, producing an output. Individual units can be used to power single buildings, and items of equipment or large scale farms can feed on to the network.

Notes

7   Show, with the aid of a diagram, how **each** of the following loads may be connected to a 400 V, four-wire supply.
a) 230 V single-phase load.
b) 400 V three-phase and neutral load.
c) 400 V three-phase balanced load.

Answer

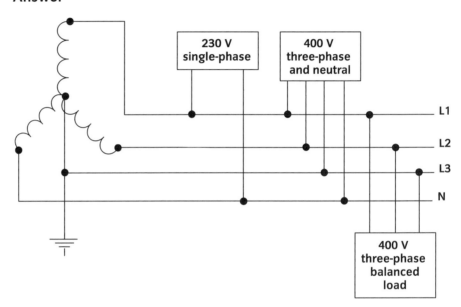

a) Between any line and neutral.
b) Connect to all three lines and neutral.
c) Connect to all three lines only.

Comments
Remember: supplies, systems and loads are still referred to as phase; it is only the conductors that are lines. The normal arrangement is to have a delta-star transformer supplied at 11 kV (three-phase) with the secondary three-phase and neutral providing a choice of voltage, nominally 400 V between any two phases and 230 V between any phase and neutral. Also between any phase and earth as the earth is connected to the neutral at the star point of the transformer. Balanced three-phase loads do not require a neutral connection.

8 Describe briefly the operating principle of a single-phase, double-wound transformer.

Answer

The current flowing in the primary produces a primary magnetic flux which circulates within the transformer core. This flux cuts the secondary coil and induces an emf in it by mutual induction.

Comments

A double-wound transformer has two separate windings which are electrically separated, the primary being connected to the supply and the secondary to the load.

9 Show, with the aid of a drawing, the layout of a three-phase Shell type transformer including the position of the primary and secondary windings.

Answer

Below is an exemplar drawing of a five-limb transformer core, having both primary and secondary windings wound on to the three central limbs.

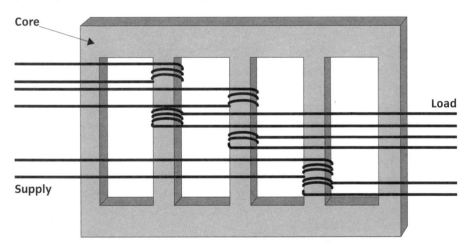

Comments

A three-phase shell transformer has three limbs for the windings, one for each phase, and two outer limbs to complete the magnetic circuit. The lower voltage winding is normally wound closest to the laminated limb for safety reasons. There are several patterns available.

Notes

10 A 20:1 step-down transformer is supplied at 230 V a.c. and has
a secondary current of 40 A. Calculate the
a) secondary voltage
b) primary current
c) transformer kVA rating.

Answer

a) Secondary voltage $= \dfrac{230}{20} = 11.5\,\text{V}$

b) Primary current $= \dfrac{40}{20} = 2\,\text{A}$

c) kVA $= \dfrac{230 \times 2}{1000} = 0.46\,\text{kVA}$

Comments

The step-down ratio of a transformer applies equally to the ratio of primary turns to secondary turns and primary voltage to secondary voltage. The current is the reverse of this. This can be seen from the formula.

$$\frac{V_P}{V_S} = \frac{N_P}{N_S} = \frac{I_S}{I_P}$$

11 An a.c. circuit consists of a coil having 30 Ω inductive reactance, a 50 Ω resistor, with a capacitor of 20 Ω capacitive reactance connected in series to a 200 V supply. Calculate the circuit current.

Answer

In order to determine the circuit current, the impedance of the circuit must be determined using

$$Z = \sqrt{R^2 + (X_L - X_C)^2} \quad \text{so}$$

$$\sqrt{50^2 + 10^2} = 50.1\,\Omega$$

and therefore the current can be determined as

$$I = \frac{V}{Z} \quad \text{then} \quad \frac{200}{50.1} = 3.99\,(4)\,\text{A}$$

Comments

A capacitor in series with an inductor will reduce the overall circuit impedance.

12 A circuit consists of a capacitor connected in series with a resistor. Draw an impedance triangle indicating the sides of the triangle representing resistance, capacitive reactance and impedance.

Answer

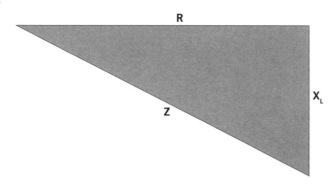

Comments

It is important to get the individual components in the correct position. Remember the voltage across the resistor is in phase with the current (horizontal line) and the voltage across the capacitor lags the current by 90°. This produces the triangle shown.

13 Explain what is meant by the terms
   a) true power
   b) apparent power
   c) reactive power.

Answer

   a) True power refers to the power actually used to do work.
   b) Apparent power is what appears to be used or taken from the supply.
   c) Reactive power is that which lags or leads the true power by 90°. It takes current but uses no power; an example of a component that produces this effect is a capacitor.

Notes

Comments

See diagram below.

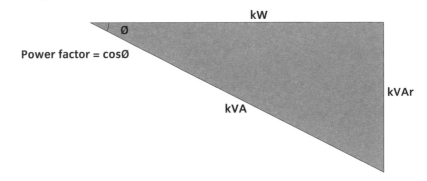

True power (kW) is the power consumed by the resistive component of the load. Apparent power is the power it appears to be consuming due to the reactive components in the circuit or load. If reactive power (kVAr) can be reduced by using components that oppose each other, such as a capacitor and resistor, the reactive power will be reduced, bringing the value of kVA to a value nearer the kW.

14 State **three** possible advantages of balancing loads across a three-phase four-wire system.

Answer

Any three from the following:
- reduces neutral current
- reduces cable size
- reduces fuse and switchgear ratings
- maximum utilisation of supply system.

Comments

If carried out on lighting circuits, within open plan areas of an installation this can also reduce stroboscopic effects produced by discharge lighting systems.

By balancing the loads over three phases the neutral current will be reduced and this also can have an effect on the rating of switchgear, control gear and distribution cables.

15 A load of 2.5 kW connected to a 230 V single-phase supply draws a current of 12 A. Calculate the power factor of the load.

Answer

$$power\ factor = \frac{W}{VA}\ then$$

$$\frac{2500}{230 \times 12} = 0.905\ or\ 0.91$$

Comments

Power factor is the ratio of true power (watts) to apparent power (VA) and has no unit as it is a ratio.

16 a) At which of the points marked A, B, C, D and E, shown in the diagram below, can power factor correction be applied for
      i) individual items of equipment
      ii) the complete installation.
    b) State the component that would be used to correct power factor in a) i) above.

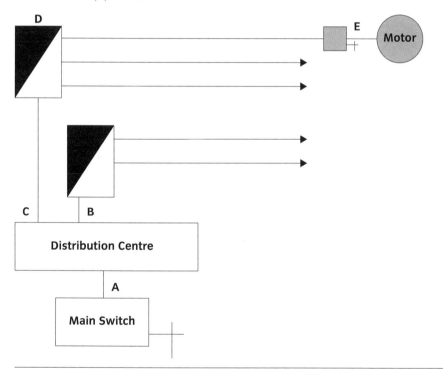

Answer

a) i)   Point E – the capacitor would be connected at the load terminals.
    ii) Point A, before the main distribution centre.
b) A capacitor.

Notes

Comments

Individual correction is achieved by connecting a capacitor at the load terminals so that the capacitor is switched with the load.

As a capacitor only corrects downstream from the point of connection then point C only corrects to the outgoing side of the distribution board.

Complete installation power factor correction is achieved by connecting a capacitor to the incoming side of the board so that an overall power factor correction is achieved. This does not correct the circuits individually, but for the installation as a whole and may need to be automatically controlled otherwise overcorrection may occur.

17 Determine, using a phasor diagram to scale, the neutral current for the following three-phase system at unity power factor
   – L1   40 A
   – L2   30 A
   – L3   20 A.

Answer

When a full phasor diagram is completed as shown in the diagram below (which is not to scale), the neutral current will be determined as 17.33 A.

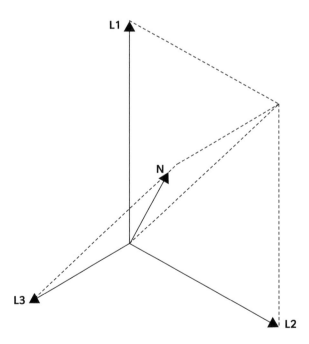

18 Calculate, using the diagram shown below, the values of the
   a) line voltage of the transformer
   b) load phase current.

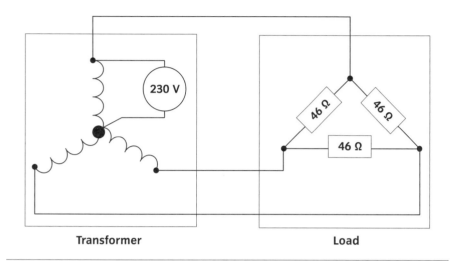

Transformer   **Load**

Answer

a) $V_L = \sqrt{3} \times V_P$ therefore $\sqrt{3} \times 230 = 400\,V$

b) $I_P\,(delta) = \dfrac{V_P}{R}$ where $V_P = V_L$ so

$\dfrac{400}{46} = 8.69\,A$

Comments

In a delta system:

Phase Voltage (V_P) = Line Voltage (V_L) and *Phase Current (I_P) = $\dfrac{Line\ Current\ (I_L)}{\sqrt{3}}$*

In a star system:

Phase Voltage (V_P) = $\dfrac{Line\ Voltage\ (V_L)}{\sqrt{3}}$ and *Phase Current (I_P) = Line Current (I_L)*

Notes

19 Draw a fully labelled circuit diagram for a d.c. shunt motor.

Answer

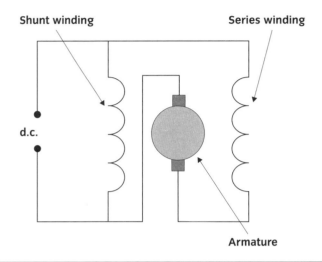

Comments

A d.c. shunt motor has the field connected in parallel with the armature.

20 Explain how starting is achieved in a capacitor start, single-phase motor.

Answer

A capacitor is connected in series with the start winding which causes a phase displacement between the magnetic fields produced by the start and run windings. A torque is produced by the interaction of these two magnetic fields.

Comments

A single-phase motor is not naturally self starting if fitted with a single set of stator windings. If a second set of stator windings is added, the rotor will simply vibrate as there is no rotating magnetic field. In order to create a rotating magnetic field the magnetic fields produced by the two windings must be displaced. A capacitor will create this phase displacement.

21 State **one** application for **each** of the following motors.
   a) Three-phase induction motor.
   b) Single-phase, capacitor start induction motor.
   c) Single-phase universal motor.

Answer
Answers may include
   a) Industrial drives such as pumps, compressors
   b) Refrigerators, compressors, central heating pumps
   c) Domestic and small industrial power tools, vacuum cleaners, drills, angle grinders.

Comments
   a) Three-phase induction motors are considered to be reliable and economical in terms of cost and efficiency. Often these motors are the preferred choice where a three-phase supply is available.
   b) These motors are commonly used within single-phase electrical equipment because they are relatively cheap, reliable and have few parts which require maintenance.
   c) Series universal motors produce a high starting torque and so are used where this characteristic is required.

22 State **one** suitable starting arrangement for **each** of the following motors.
   a) 3 kW single-phase induction motor.
   b) 25 kW three-phase induction motor.
   c) 20 kW three-phase, wound rotor induction motor.

Answer
   a) Typically a direct-on-line starter.
   b) Star-delta starter **or** a soft start arrangement.
   c) Rotor resistance starter.

Comments
   a) Small motors would normally be controlled by a DOL starter as the starting current is low and the DOL starter is relatively cheap to install.
   b) Large three phase induction motors have a high starting current which must be controlled. Star-delta and soft-starts are an effective way of controlling the currents involved.
   c) This motor is designed to be controlled using a rotor resistance starter.

23 Describe the operation of a DOL starter, controlling a small milling machine, when the supply voltage to the starter is briefly interrupted.

Answer

On the loss of supply voltage the hold-in circuit of the contactor coil is de-energised and the contacts open, disconnecting the supply to the machine. Restarting can only be initiated manually.

Comments

This type of control is necessary where automatic re-starting of the machine may cause danger. This action is referred to as 'undervoltage protection'.

24 Explain which component parts cause the operation of a 6A, 30 mA RCBO, protecting a circuit when a
a) current of 30 mA flows to earth in the circuit
b) short circuit current flows in the circuit.

Answer

a) The 30 mA earth fault current causes the RCD component to operate and disconnect the circuit.
b) The magnetic component (instantaneous tripping mechanism) of the circuit breaker will operate and disconnect the supply.

Comments

RCDs can only detect an out of balance between the line and neutral currents.

The circuit breaker component detects overcurrents between line and neutral which are not detected by the RCD.

The RCBO combines both these functions in a single device.

25 The illuminance on a surface 4 m directly below a lamp is 200 lux. Determine the level of illuminance on the surface if the lamp is moved 2 metres closer to the surface.

Answer

$E = \dfrac{I}{d^2}$ therefore

$I = E \times d^2$ so $I = 200 \times 4^2 = 3200$ candella (cd) therefore

E at new point $= \dfrac{3200}{2^2} = 800$ lux

Comments

You need to have an understanding of the Inverse Square Law and Cosine Law as applied to point-to-point lighting calculations. An area 1 m^2 on a surface 1 m immediately below a lamp emitting light equally in all directions will have an illuminance of one lux. If this distance is doubled then the same number of lumens has to illuminate an area four times greater (4 m^2) so each receives a quarter of the previous value.

26 a) Explain why compact fluorescent lamps may be selected in preference to GLS lamps.
    b) State **one** disadvantage of using low pressure sodium vapour lamps.

Answer

a) Compact fluorescent lamps are more energy efficient, having a higher efficacy (lumen per watt output) than GLS lamps.
b) The light output from a low pressure sodium vapour lamp gives poor colour rendering.

Comments

The efficacy of a luminaire is given by the number of lumens produced per watt of power consumed. With discharge lamps this would include the power consumed by the control gear.

27 Describe, with the aid of a diagram, how the process of convection is used to heat a room using a wall-mounted electric heater.

Answer

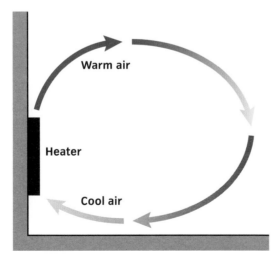

As warm air rises from the heater, heating the room, the cooler air is drawn into the heater, which in turn is heated. This rotating airflow continues, heating the room.

Notes

28 Explain the function of the following components when used in heating systems.
a) Time switch.
b) Frost thermostat (frost-stat).
c) Contactor.

Answer
a) A time switch is used to turn loads on and off at set times.
b) A frost thermostat is used to detect low ambient temperatures in order to turn on heating systems, overriding other controls, and so prevent damage due to low temperatures, such as freezing pipes.
c) A contactor is used to switch loads on and off which have a current rating greater than the capacity of thermostats, time switches, etc.

Comments
a) The name 'time switch' describes its action controlling the operation of the system to suit the user's requirements.
b) A frost-stat is simply a thermostat which is used to detect low temperatures. If the main heating system is switched off there is a risk of the building fabric being damaged should the temperature drop to around 0°C. In this case the frost-stat would override the main control and bring the heating back on.
c) A contactor has the capacity to switch large currents. Many time switches and thermostats are only rated at around 6 A, so would be incapable of switching large heating loads. The low current contactor coil is controlled by the programmer or thermostat and in turn the main contacts of the contactor switch the larger load.

29 State the function of a
a) thermistor in a domestic heating control system
b) thermistor in a motor winding
c) photodiode in a passive infra-red detector.

Answer
a) It is used to detect changes in the temperature of air or water to control a heating system.
b) It detects overheating in the windings and then disconnect the motor to prevent damage.
c) It is used to detect changes in light patterns caused by movement.

30 State **one** typical electronic application for **each** of the following components.
a) Diode.
b) Triac.
c) Thyristor.

Answer
a) A standard diode will commonly be used in a rectifier.
b) Speed controllers, dimmers on a.c. circuits.
c) Used for motor speed controls and power switching.

Comments
a) Other types of diodes include light emitting diodes (LED), photodiodes and zener diodes.
b) A triac is a four element device. It will conduct in either direction when triggered and is therefore used on a.c circuits.
c) A thyristor is a rectifier which can be switched on, and when fitted with a second gate, switched off. It only conducts in one direction.

Notes

Notes

More information

More information

Notes

Further reading

BS 7671: 2008 Requirements for Electrical Installations, IEE Wiring Regulations Seventeenth Edition, published by the IEE, London, 2008

On-Site Guide: BS 7671: 2008, published by the IEE, London, 2008

The Electrician's Guide to Good Electrical Practice, published by Amicus, 2008

Electrician's Guide to the Building Regulations, published by the IEE, London, 2nd Edition 2008

IEE Guidance Notes, a series of guidance notes, each of which expands upon and amplifies the particular requirements of a part of the IEE Wiring Regulations, Seventeenth Edition, published by the IEE, London:
– Guidance Note 1: *Selection and Erection of Equipment*, 5th Edition 2009
– Guidance Note 2: *Isolation and Switching*, 5th Edition 2009
– Guidance Note 3: *Inspection and Testing*, 5th Edition 2008
– Guidance Note 4: *Protection Against Fire*, 5th Edition 2009
– Guidance Note 5: *Protection Against Electric Shock*, 5th Edition 2009
– Guidance Note 6: *Protection Against Overcurrent*, 5th Edition 2009
– Guidance Note 7: *Special Locations*, 3rd Edition 2009
– Guidance Note 8: *Earthing and Bonding*, 2007

Brian Scaddan, *Electrical Installation Work*, published by Newnes, 2008

John Whitfield, *Electrical Craft Principles, Volumes 1 and 2*, published by the IEE, London, 2009

Online resources

Notes

City & Guilds www.cityandguilds.com
The City & Guilds website can give you more information about studying for further professional and vocational qualifications to advance your personal or career development, as well as locations of centres that provide the courses.

SmartScreen www.smartscreen.co.uk
City & Guilds' dedicated online support portal SmartScreen provides learner and tutor support for over 100 City & Guilds qualifications. It helps engage learners in the excitement of learning and enables tutors to free up more time to do what they love the most – teach!

Institution of Engineering and Technology (IET) www.theiet.org
The Institution of Engineering and Technology was formed by the amalgamation of the Institution of Electrical Engineers (IEE) and the Institution of Incorporated Engineers (IIE). It is the largest professional engineering society in Europe and the second largest of its type in the world. The Institution produces the IEE Wiring Regulations and a range of supporting material and courses.

British Standards Institution www.bsi-global.com

CORGI Services Ltd www.trustcorgi.com

ELECSA Ltd www.elecsa.org.uk

Electrical Contractors' Association (ECA) www.eca.co.uk

Joint Industry Board for the Electrical Contracting Industry (JIB)
www.jib.org.uk

NAPIT Certification Services Ltd www.napit.org.uk

National Inspection Council for Electrical Installation Contracting (NICEIC) www.niceic.org.uk

Oil Firing Technical Association for the Petroleum Industry (OFTEC)
www.oftec.co.uk

Further courses

City & Guilds Level 3 Certificate in the Requirements for Electrical Installations BS 7671: 2008 (2382-10)

This qualification is aimed at practising electricians with relevant experience and is intended to ensure that they are conversant with the format, content and application of BS 7671: Requirements for Electrical Installations, 17th Edition.

City & Guilds Level 2 Certificate in Fundamental Inspection, Testing and Initial Verification (2392-10)

This qualification provides candidates with an introduction to the initial verification of electrical installations. It is aimed at practising electricians who have not carried out inspection and testing since qualifying, those who require update training and those with limited experience of inspection and testing. Together with suitable on-site experience, it also prepares candidates to go on to the Level 3 certificate (2391-10).

City & Guilds Level 3 Certificate in Inspection, Testing and Certification of Electrical Installations (2391-10)

This course is aimed at those with practical experience of inspection and testing of LV electrical installations, who need to become certificated. It is not suitable for beginners. In addition to relevant practical experience, candidates must possess a good working knowledge of the requirements of BS 7671 to City & Guilds Level 3 certificate standard or equivalent.

City & Guilds Level 3 Certificate in the Code of Practice for In-Service Inspection and Testing of Electrical Equipment (2377)

This course, commonly known as PAT/Portable Appliance Testing, is for staff undertaking and recording inspection and testing of electrical equipment. The course includes a practical exercise. Topics covered include equipment construction, inspection and recording, combined inspection and testing, and equipment.

City & Guilds Level 3 Certificate in the Building Regulations for Electrical Installations in Dwellings (2393-10)

The primary aim of this qualification is to enable practising electricians, operating in the domestic environment, to gain an understanding of how electrical installations in dwellings must comply with all relevant Building Regulations. It is suitable for those working in the building trades and others who require a working knowledge of how electrical installations in dwellings can affect the building construction.

JIB Electrotechnical Certification Scheme (ECS) Health and Safety Assessment

This Health and Safety Assessment is a requirement for electricians wishing to work on larger construction projects and sites in the UK and the exam is an online type very similar in format to the GOLA tests. It is now a mandatory requirement for holding an ECS card, and is a requirement for all members of the ECS. Please refer to www.jib.org.uk/ecs2.htm for details.

Notes

Notes